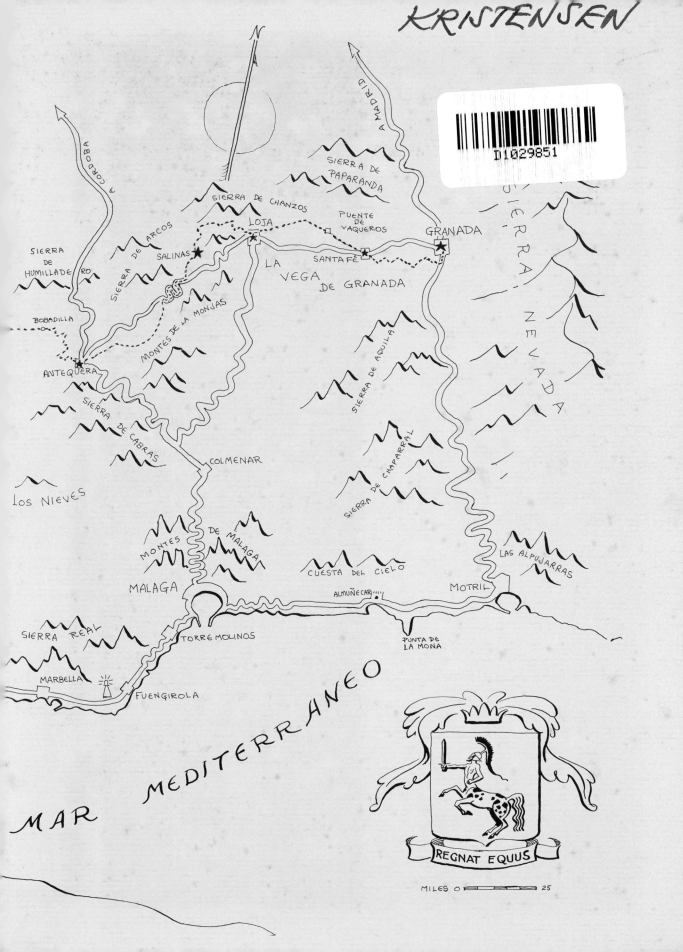

MAR MEDITERRANEO

MAR

REGNAT EQUUS

MILES 0 ⟷ 25

# Long Ride to Granada

# Long Ride to
# GRANADA

✿✿✿✿✿✿✿✿✿✿✿✿✿✿✿✿✿✿✿✿✿✿✿✿✿✿✿✿✿✿✿✿✿✿✿✿✿✿✿✿✿✿✿✿

*by James Bodrero*

REYNAL & COMPANY, INC.

*New York, 1965*

*This book is for C.O. and G. B.*

Una dama sujerio la cabalgata,
otra la hizo posible;
a las dos cariñosamente,
les dedicó este libro.

W E CRESTED THE PASS and stopped to rest the horses. From here the trail twisted dizzily down to Arcos de la Frontera. Far below the city snaked the dusty motor road I had once taken; then I was plodding with the herd—now I was riding with the eagles!

On the far horizon great goblin clouds loomed over the Spanish mountains toward Ronda, still days away. From time to time we had passed bands of gypsies, like some wild animals, deer or sheep perhaps, driving across the passes, straight as arrows, heading from one fair to the next. They, born to these wilds, had known the shortest ways before they knew how to button their pants, or had pants to button.

Around the mountain's shoulder rattled a high-wheeled country cart, tandem as always, two mules, one large wheeler and a smaller leader.

7

"*Con Dios, caballeros* [Go with God, horsemen]." The driver gave us the courteous salutation we were to hear over and over again during the following weeks. We were tracing the hoofprints made a hundred and thirty-five years ago by Washington Irving when he rode three hundred miles across the mountains to his first sight of Granada.

"*Vaya con Dios*," we answered. This greeting in the high mountains has a meaning more serious than mere politeness, for here in the high passes, through the great valleys between these ancient and forgotten cities, one needs God's blessing to safely complete a journey.

As the tandem of mules to the high-wheeled country cart went up the drovers' road, the *camino vaquero*, I thought of the tandems, the sporting tandems of my youth. You are the last of the Edwardians, I thought, you romantic old horse-loving anachronism; here in the wild Sierras of Spain chasing a lost youth in a reconstruction of another man's hundred-and-thirty-five-year-old voyage. Signaling to my companions, I headed down.

Now I am past my prime and only on a horse completely myself. When young, a man completes himself in many ways, but when time catches up a good horse bolsters the old man's ego as nothing else any longer can. This is not supposed to be a lecture but a notebook of a trip, so I mustn't diverge too much, but these were my thoughts as I rode along easily on this good *caballo* across one of the most beautiful passes in Spain. They may help to explain my being there that day.

The fact of belonging to a generation that rode horses not only in sport but to exist, to go to school, to visit friends and to work, has much to do with it. I learned a love of horses that has become a welcome constant in my life. This may be my last long ride, but to the end I hope there will be at least a good round-trotting pony to a trap.

8

For the last five years I have been living in this lovely land of Spain, in Andalucía, full of almost every quality that I have learned to respect, including its fine horses and fine horsemanship. I long wanted a good excuse to do a ride of this sort; then in Granada a year ago I reread a book and my voyage was given meaning.

When during my school days I first read Washington Irving's *Tales of the Alhambra* I am sure I must have skipped the introduction; it is a sort of dedication to his companion, Prince Dolgurouky, the Russian minister at that time stationed in Madrid. This introduction, called "The Journey," described the ride of these two adventurous young men who, in Irving's words, decided ". . . to wander together among the romantic mountains of Andalusia." This fired my imagination.

The Spain that most visitors become familiar with is that which is covered by two great touring loops, one to the north and one to the south of Madrid. The first leads north through La Gránja, Segovia, Valladolid and Burgos to the Basque country and San Sebastian; one can return by way of Bilbao, Santander, Gijón, Oviedo, Leon, Zamora, Salamanca and Avila, and so back to Madrid, a most fascinating journey. The southern route covering all of Andalucía leads through Valdepeñas to Córdoba, Sevilla, Jerez, Algeciras, Marbella, Málaga, Granada and back to Madrid via Jaén, Bailén and Aránjuez, where one can sit at an outdoor restaurant by the riverbank and, in the spring, enjoy the finest *fraises de bois* and asparagus in the world.

Both of these journeys are immensely rewarding, for they cover almost all of Spain's great monuments, both artistic and architectural; from them one enjoys a complete conception of this ancient and historic land. But it is away from these roads, far from the centers of "Gran-Turismo," that another Spain emerges.

Well do I remember Tordesillas from whose monastery the mad queen, Juana la Loca, daughter of Ferdinand and Isabella, ruled

Spain for over forty years. That day we were the only visitors in the city, and while my wife played on Juana's little harmonium, still in tune, in the convent's courtyard I watched the old caretaker training a young falcon. In Oropesa one spends the night in a Gothic castle taken over by the government as a *parador* or stopping place. During the centuries of Moorish wars a Christian girl from this castle was captured by the Moors, who offered to return her inviolate for her weight in gold. This was done, and the town changed its name to Oropesa, meaning weight of gold in the feminine, and redesigned its coat of arms to show a girl sitting on a scale. In the courtyard of this castle, which is quite small, two bulls were once fought by the great Peruvian *rejoneadora* Conchita Cintrón, an amazing feat when one considers the restricted space she worked in. That I would have loved to have seen.

Consider Pastrana, only half a day's journey over an incredibly bad road from Madrid. Seldom visited except by museum directors, this tiny hamlet houses the greatest early-Renaissance tapestries in the world. King Philip II's first wife, a Portuguese, brought these great tapestries to Spain as part of her dowry; they represent her father's victories over the Moors and now hang in the little local church. The history of their arrival in their present location is interesting and a bit scandalous. Philip, sometime after his wife's death, gave them to his Italian mistress, the Princess of Eboli. This lovely lady, apparently bored with her royal lover, was eventually caught in bed with his chamberlain, a disastrous lack of discretion! The fate of the indiscrete gentleman has to be imagined; he simply disappears from history, while she, as was customary, was banished to a nunnery.

Being who she was, she was not condemned to be a simple nun but was allowed to build herself a sumptuous monastery at Pastrana over which she ruled as abbess. There is a charming picture of her in the church, semi-nude, being divested of her jewels be-

11

fore taking holy orders. The tapestries she of course took with her to decorate her new abode and on her death left them to the parish church. It is interesting that no one, the state or the bishopric of Gualalajara, has the power to take these tapestries away from the little village church whose property they are. This hamlet is so rural it doesn't even have a restaurant; in fact, a visitor has to bring his lunch in a basket. Talking to the priest in its dusty little square, I told him how surprised I was that Pastrana, humble as it was, could still control one of the great art treasures of the world.

"Don Jaime," he answered proudly, "we are perhaps in many ways as poor a town as you can find in Spain; as you see, we are only shepherds, but we are able to boast two things: the tapestries and the best football team in the province, of which, pardon me, I may say I am the coach. Señor, when one is limited one prizes all the more the little that one has." Only twice have they ever been removed—once for safety during the civil war, and once to go to the great exhibition of tapestries held some years ago in Bordeaux. So there is no way to see one of the world's greatest art treasures except by taking that long and dusty journey. Very few do.

Among other interesting places are, for instance, Vejer, not far from Cape Trafalgar, where the women still go completely veiled with only one eye showing, obviously a custom remaining from Moorish days. Medina-Sidonia, towering on its mountain peak on a back road halfway between Algeciras and Jerez, means, to an Englishman, the Admiral of the Spanish Armada, but the original city was burned by Scipio Africanus who went on to found Itálica near Seville, named for his mother. One of the most sumptuous of Roman residential suburbs, this town was the birthplace of Seneca and the two Spanish emperors, Trajan and Hadrian. It has a very beautiful and smallish amphitheater. I wondered while wandering in it if they ever had announcements in those days such as this:

## MAGNIFICENT CORRIDA OF BARBARIANS

21             Barbarians of Julio Orso            21

to be destroyed by

### These Well-known and Popular Lions

IMPERATOR, TRIUMPHATOR II, FURIOSO

*Tickets at all Wine Shops*                 *5 Cestercii*

No doubt there was something of that sort to entertain the populace.

All Andalucía was Roman at one time, held by a line of forts which became towns and cities ringing the mountain frontiers. On the sea beyond Málaga still stands the great Roman fort of Almuñécar, to give it the Moorish name it now has. This was the headquarters of the Sixth Legion, commanded by one of the forebears of a friend of mine, Alfredo di Carpegna, in his time European champion at auto racing, golf and tennis. This legion controlled the great fisheries, still one of the richest in the Mediterranean, from which all the Roman legions were fed, for, if you remember, the daily ration of a Roman soldier was a dried fish and his helmet full of corn. Everything else he had to get off the country.

Behind these ancient towns lie even older mysteries, for from these mountains, originating of course somewhere in Africa, moved the 'dark men who, gradually growing lighter through the ages, the sun worshipers, the dolmen builders, eventually left us their apotheosis in Stonehenge.

The Romans gave way to the Gothic kings; they in turn fell to the Moors who, after seven hundred years, gave way to Ferdinand and Isabella. Their ancient towns still stand and they called me.

13

Cut off by time and new auto routes, they still lie sleeping, a hundred years back in customs, a fair goal for an old man seeking the quieter life of his youth.

The *posadas,* those old Spanish caravansaries, have existed for hundreds of years in these remote areas and will still give shelter to man and beast. The trails, mule tracks, *camino vaqueros* and jeep roads crisscrossed the Sierras; so far as possible I would follow "The Journey" and see what remained a hundred and thirty-five years after they rode off to Granada.

Admitted, primarily it was my love of horses that inspired this ride rather than a profound interest in Irving's journey. Had it been necessary to make the trip by car I doubt that I should have been so enthusiastic. So first I will talk about the horses, the Spanish horses which I have come so to admire.

A horse is after all man-made; just as an automobile is designed for its purpose—racing, trucking, passenger carrying—so a horse is bred and then trained to answer a given purpose. In the field of manners, as a saddle horse the Spaniard has found the answer as no one else today excepting a few, a very few, old California *paisanos,* and they are fast dying out.

Remember that the highest degree of horse management is arrived at in the Spanish Riding School in Vienna—aptly named, for its art is Spanish—and the trained Lippizaners that amaze all who see them are carrying out to the ultimate that manège that all good Spanish riding horses acquire to a lesser degree.

On most well-broken horses in Spain you do not ride on but with them. They are taught not only to obey but to entertain. You enjoy them, you feel the pleasant companionship of their easy gait, the intelligent effort to please, the conversation telegraphed by bit to bridle to hand, the response to knee and thigh and balance so willingly given that these friends can never bore you.

In Spain, as in our Western States, horses are usually ridden in a light-curb bit alone. This I find is always the finest connection between a sensitive mouth and a sensitive hand. A snaffle may have its place on the track or in the hunting field, but the finest affinity between horse and rider is a light curb hardly used at all. Then riding a gay horse can be like dancing with a lovely girl!

The highest degree of Spanish horsemanship today is to be seen in the art of *rejonear* or the fighting of bulls from horseback. In this act the three phases of the fight on foot are duplicated by the horseman, beautifully mounted, who ends the *faena* by a lance thrust, failing which he dismounts and kills the bull on foot.

The Spanish word *rejonear* comes from the word *rejón* or lance. Two types of *rejón* are used. The first, the *rejón de castigo,* takes the place of the pic, which in the hands of a picador punishes the bull's neck and shoulder muscles, causing him to lower his head and charge straight. These strokes must be delivered with the bull charging and the horse at a dead run and never being submitted

to danger of the horns. This calls for extremes of horse management.

After two or three of these punishing attacks, interspersed with very close offering and evasions of the bull's charges, the rider changes horses and comes out for the second *suerte* or phase of the *banderillas*.

In this *suerte* the finest *rejoneadors* take a *banderilla* or barbed stick in each hand and ride their horses with knee control alone. Facing the bull across the plaza, the horseman, by rearing and cavorting his horse, always without reins, incites the bull's charge and then at full speed meets him face to face and with knee pressure at the last moment evades the bull while planting the *banderillas* in his shoulders. After two or three pairs of sticks, one or two of the very finest practitioners of the art even finish by planting in the bull's crest a rose fastened to a tiny dart. The degree of horsemanship required for this last act, the closeness with which the bull has to be worked, can hardly be imagined.

Changing horses again, the *rejoneador* takes up the *rejón de*

*muerte* or lance of death. This lance is of the same length as the first one, about four and a half feet, and is used in one hand like a dagger. In this case, instead of a short blade, it has one about two and a half feet long. Citing as before, the horse and the bull charge together, as the Spaniards say, *frente a frente,* or face to face. Properly placed between the shoulder blades, driven with the combined force of the two charging animals, this lance will kill.

The degree of skill required of both horse and rider are beyond belief in this most beautiful and dangerous of all horse exercises that I have ever seen. You will find here, under desperate conditions, put to use most of the maneuvers that in Vienna are carried out to music.

The great majority of these riders are gentlemen amateurs such as the Alvaro Domecqs, father and son, Don Fermín Bohorquez, Don Salvador Guardiola, one of the richest young men in Spain, killed in the ring at Palma de Majorca three years ago, and the two great professionals, the Peralta brothers. The amateurs, most of whom are breeders, fight for local charities in the towns in which they appear.

To me it is the most beautiful and bravest exhibition of equestrian art to be seen in the world today.

One of Spain's great centers of horsemanship is Jerez de la Frontera, so to Jerez, home of all fine sherry, I went to find my horses. This city is the home of horses and horsemen and of the latter one family stands out, the Domecqs. I am proud to count them my friends, and the closest, José Ignacio—great polo player, great horseman and, best of all, a friend whose kindness finds no limit in his willingness to be imposed upon—it was to him I turned.

His experience led me into the capable hands of Don Manuel Delgado, an Andalucian gentleman of Jerez who deals skillfully, lovingly and honestly in horses. My wants were seven horses, four saddle horses, three packers, and two vaqueros to handle them.

Delgado, on his ranch outside Jerez, put together a perfect *remuda* of mounts; good traveling horses with a lot of blood in them and a fine free way of going. The three pack horses, also fast walkers and joggers, were well selected so as not to hold us back. As Don José Ignacio had predicted, "Delgado will find you the very best of mounts and men."

The first choice and *mayoral* or foreman was José Burgo Ramirez, a typical son of Andalucía, twenty-three years old, but looking at least thirty from a life of hard riding and responsibility; handsome, slight, of medium height, a horseman of immense skill and experience, he was Delgado's foreman, detached for this trip as a favor to Domecq. I have never met a man anywhere more horse-wise and mountainwise, so exactly suited to his job.

Antonio Pérez Fernández, a year older, was a taller, slighter copy of the first; raised from childhood with stock, the son of José Ignacio Domecq's *mayoral,* he was lent by that openhanded friend to make our way easier. He was much less serious than Burgo and along the trail a pleasant singer of the lighter *cante alegrías,* a good companion.

Burgo rode a young bay thoroughbred called Agrilijo, such a fast walker that we soon learned never to let him set the pace. Antonio rode a crossbred, Arab-Spanish horse called Banderas. My horse, Bejeriegos, was a dark bay, dock-tailed Anglo-Arab about fifteen two in height, a very fine and easy goer. The three pack horses, Gasolina, Moras and El Pony were all sturdy Spanish-Arab crosses, and the last horse, a very handsome bay thoroughbred, Marleños, was for my companion Gregory McIntosh.

This young friend of twenty-five until now was best known as one of America's finest underwater photographers. He had worked for the Smithsonian in the Florida Keys and the Bahamas during the discovery and salvaging of artifacts from H.M.S. *Looe,* a cruiser that went down with a captured privateer in tow in the eighteenth century. Greg, who comes of a horsy family in Warrenton, Virginia, decided, to my gratification, to exchange the bends for saddle sores and become my companion. Colloquial in Spanish, a good horseman with a quick, perceptive eye, Greg was a perfect addition to our small cavalcade. Humorous, always thoughtful and courageous, I couldn't have wished for a more pleasant comrade.

Usually one finds that the equipment and clothing most suitable for any given purpose is that designed and developed by the local conditions; so Greg and I had *traje corto,* the local high-waisted, short-jacketed cowboy clothes made by the tailor at Estepona who furnished most of the local vaqueros. They were of tough gray twill and represented the blue jean pants and jumper of the Western cowboy.

We carried a change of shirts, riding trousers and long-John underwear; sufficient, as overnight washing could be had anywhere. Soft boots, rough side out, and a *sombrero ancho* or flat-brimmed Córdobés hat completed the outfit. Around the waist was tied a large twisted silk handkerchief, which by modern fashion takes the place of the old-time sash.

The whole costume is referred to as *campero,* or countryman's, and is light and useful, workmanlike, not gaudy or showy.

We carried socks, handkerchiefs, a few paperbacks, toilet articles, lighter fluid, Greg's cameras and equipment and my sketching things; Greg had a sweater, I a quilted windbreaker cut short like the *corto* jacket. These were most welcome morning and evening in the mountains. We also had saddle-slickers which we never needed; we were able to pack in a pair of saddlebags and a small duffle bag apiece.

We took bedrolls and enough cooking equipment to heat up soup, a pot of coffee, or some bacon of a morning. These were to prove absolutely unnecessary and could have saved us the use of at least one pack horse. Actually the only things we ever used

from the packs, barring our personal dunnage, were the first-aid kit and a bottle of tabasco sauce!

I didn't realize then that with *posadas* in every little town, augmented by small wayside *cantinas*, the back country of Spain is fully prepared to serve the needs of the great numbers of mounted travelers who, by horse, mule and burro, still journey daily through this enchanted land.

Well, all this gear was finally collected in Jerez; one afternoon we moved it to Don Manuel's *finca* and sorted it into equal packs. We said good-by to José Ignacio Domecq, who was off to Argentina on a business trip, and called an early start for the following day.

So on the fifth of October, in lovely sunny autumn weather, we swung up and rode out of Delgado's and started the long ride from Jerez up over the rolling downs toward the high Sierras where three hundred miles away lay Granada, at the end of our Spanish cavalcade.

Our first day's stage, a long gradual climb, led us to the fabled mountain city of Arcos de la Frontera, perched high on a cliff overhanging the valley of the Rio Guadalete.

All day long we slowly rode higher, mesa succeeding mesa, each long low grade imperceptibly lifting us; it was only looking back trail that we noticed we were climbing all the time. Most of this land, until two years ago cattle country, now is planted to cotton fields. These stretch to the horizons on either side. Far ahead of us was our immediate goal, a gun-sight notch in the Sierra del Calvario. Through that distant gateway lay Arcos.

The Spanish are trying to make themselves independent of Egyptian cotton and with government encouragement are rapidly developing a cotton industry of good size. Modern progress is to be commended, but this particular example led to a bad moment for us.

Burgo had been using a well in one of the high passes for many years in his travels through these mountains, and in the middle

of the long hot afternoon we arrived, tired and thirsty, under its welcoming yoke. Standing in the middle of the endless cotton fields was a cement watering trough leading from the wellhead, from which it was fed by a sluice into which one emptied a hand bucket on a block and tackle. The horses all lined up at the empty trough and Antonio, climbing up the wellhead, began hoisting and bailing water into the sluice. The horses eagerly started sucking almost as fast as he could bail, so there was never over three inches of water in the trough.

We were standing around, stretching our legs and waiting our turn at the bucket, when a big hard-looking man on a tall Roman-nosed horse came cantering in and saluted Burgo courteously.

"Good day, friend, and to all."

"To you, Obregon, as always."

"I bring a sad request, good gentlemen . . ."

And so on and on with the usual Spanish honorifics and politeness; in short, please stop watering the horses and in future . . . But Burgo had long used the well . . . Admitted, but the changing times . . . Times?

"Old friend, the water, alas, now belongs to the cotton. My orders you understand, not my desire . . ."

We batted the ball of politeness back and forth till we got all the horses watered, then thanking him sarcastically for nothing, mounted and rode off.

We left him standing sadly by the well.

Progress.

The hours passed hotter and drier as we kept riding upward. Finally leaving the cotton fields and winding through high, scattered groves of olives and into the pine trees, the road became a narrow trail, the pines more tortured and wind-blown. Breasting the height, we at last came through the notch and found how high we really had climbed. At our feet lay that fantastic mountain city,

24

castle-crowned, Roman, Arab and Gothic, garlanded with circling eagles, Arcos de la Frontera.

The city, clinging to its sheer cliff a thousand feet above the river, like most fortified places dates back to prehistoric times. Man has always moved into naturally secure positions. The Iberians first dug the caves which cut straight through to the precipice, in which we were to stable our horses. The Romans came and fortified it and from Arcos controlled the traffic and threw their influence over a wide area. Goths, ravaging down from the north when the Empire fell, took over, left their stamp, and in their turn gave way to the great Arab invasion of Europe. For seven hundred years, during which even Baghdad was administered by the Caliphate of Córdoba, these, by Dark Age standards civilized geniuses, laid their culture over the older ones. This is why the topmost battlements of the castle of the Dukes of Arcos are Arab crenelated.

Finally in 1264, two hundred years before Granada fell and Columbus was able to sail, came the Reconquista under King Alfonso X, "El Sabio," the Wise. Ruling from Sevilla, he had taken Jerez, San Lucar and Rota (the great U.S. Naval Base), with "fifty caballeros [knights] from Sevilla, all of them carefully named and those under them, the subjection of Arcos of the Frontier . . . was accomplished by the Grace of God and to his Glory."

It is one of the most beautifully situated and preserved medieval monuments in the world and because of its remoteness one of the least visited. No Tourist or Better-Business Bureau is there to welcome you, only a very primitive hotel and a *posada* or caravansary where we stayed; our horses stabled in a great cave with windows cut through the living stone overlooking the river, we in an ancient house built above it on three levels.

There isn't even one guide in this unique and lovely city. However, they do provide, out of their immense archeological and architectural treasure, five postcards.

Our entry at dusk into the narrow, steep, slick cobbled streets of this ancient stronghold gave us our first taste of what two days later could have been tragic. Slipping and sliding, coasting half the time, we finally skidded through the great arch into the stable-cave of the "Posada de las Cuevas." This cave was divided into stalls, and storerooms for travelers' packs and baggage. Whole pack-trains used to shelter here and the huge place was well occupied by the horses of visiting farmers, though camions have driven the old *arrieros* and their mule pack-trains off the roads. From here winding stairs cut into the mountain led up to the inn which rambled around for about three storeys. There we were soon comfortably settled for the night.

Arcos is famous all over Andalucía for its classic gypsy singing and dancing. It is the home of the true flamenco, and I had heard a few of their finest artists in other places. Wanting to enjoy them in their own setting, we made a few inquiries after dinner. Alas, the *feria* or fair had just ended; everyone was either too tired, hungover, broke, or all three, and, far from any spontaneous gaiety, the town folded up by midnight when an Andaluz city is usually just coming to life. So, no *cante jondo,* no ecstatic *gitanas,* no hammering guitars.

That night there was a full moon over Arcos; it silvered the old tiled roofs, picked out a stork's nest across the narrow crooked street from the Posada de las Cuevas, and silhouetted the towering castle keep.

Greg and I were enjoying a last cigarette on the terrace outside our rooms when we heard far away in the lower town a voice raised in *cante jondo,* the "Ay . . . ay . . . e . . . e" of a singer calling upon his tragic *sueño,* what Walter Starkie called racial consciousness; after a very few tentative phrases it stopped. The *tocaor* or guitarist, trying to sense the singer's, the *cantaors's,* mood, improvised softly, inquiringly, leading the singer in search of his *duende,* his inspiration; personal demon, the gypsies say.

This probing musical exploration can go on for hours. We were too tired to search for the *zambra*—the flamenco song feast.

Instead we lazily recalled other nights of *cante flamenco*.

For hours I have seen Beni de Cádiz sit just watching his hands, or eyes shut tight, his face working agonizingly, trying to find his *duende* with the help of a lightly touched guitar. Suddenly a spark catches, lights some hidden flame!

Trancelike, the singer stiffens and, beginning with a wail, "Ay, ay . . . e . . . e . . ." the *siguiriya gitana* pours out (Starkie again) "not mere natural suffering but a vague, everlasting pessimism—a tragic sense of life."

Immediately the guitarist stops or simply raps with his fingers on the instrument, the gypsy, "biting the song," swings his tones higher and higher; his rendition becomes more ecstatic.

It is in this waiting for inspiration, this insistence on not singing until carried away, that the gypsy differs from all others in his presentation. A gypsy is not performing; he is expressing. The song is not memorized and seldom written, but improvised. The mood is there, developed by a yearning inspired by the guitar, and finally forced out when his *duende* takes absolute possession of him.

Gradually this trancelike state communicates itself to the listeners. They too are swept up into the singer's personal fantasy. So the mood is set. First the music, then the song, and last the dance. That is the order of importance that the gypsies give to the flamenco expression as a whole.

In the same way flamenco dancers, under true conditions, never jump up and dance on cue. You will see them, men standing, women seated, intently concentrating, heads bowed, eyes shut, hands clapping softly, *palmas sordas,* for a true gypsy never uses castanets; only the hand and finger snap, waiting for the spirit to take possession of them.

Suddenly carried away, a man or woman can no longer resist

28

the expression of the dance! Now the rhythmic handclaps become louder, the guitars pick it up, and the dancer surrenders to emotion. As the dance progresses the singer, carried away, may break in again, singing now to the dancer. This triple inspiration from music to singer to dancer and back again, *tocaor, cantaor, bailar,* weaves in and out throughout a typical *noche flamenco.*

Walter Starkie, who wrote "SPAIN, a Musician's Journey through Time and Space," the definitive book on the flamenco, said, "When Manuel Torres rose to the full climax of Cante Jondo with its inner tragedy, forcing the notes higher and higher, the guitar produced a similar metallic tone to that of the singer. And when the latter's voice faltered or his inspiration began to flag, the guitar would broaden out into a bewildering series of 'falsetas' or variations, for its function . . . was the duty of sustaining the singer, enabling him to dissolve in sadness in the funereal dirge or arouse himself to a mad climax of joy . . . the guitar has been called "the conscience of Andalucía." The guitarist creates the atmosphere for the singer and the background enables him to find scope for his inspiration.

You have only to see a sensitive guitarist watching his singer's face, trying to catch his slightest change of mood, perhaps teasing him, leading him on, or dropping back to a thoughtful plucking of chords, to realize the enormous importance of this instrument in skillful hands, to understand that the guitarist is the amalgam that binds the parts into a complete whole.

The mood of a *quadro flamenco* can change with startling suddenness, for different dancers as the frenzy possesses them will express their personal *duende* in different ways, from the tragic *siguiriya* to the wild *buleria.* The whole group, volatile, changes and supports each new inspiration. The accompaniment of rhythmic hand clapping is interspersed with approving *"Olés"* or cries of *"Morena"* or *"Faraona,"* meaning Moorish girl or daughter of Pharaoh, naturally admiring references to an African origin. You

Bodrero '64

3

Bodreno '60

don't know what the term "letting down her hair" really means until you have seen a frenzied *gitana* such as La Chi Chi, carried away by her dance, shake herself loose from her careful coiffure, scattering combs and flowers all around her as her hair cascades over her face!

However, our reminiscent mood conjured up no *noche flamenco* here in Arcos. Our tentative guitarist had fallen silent; the moon was low. Tired and a little saddle-weary, Greg and I at last turned in.

The following day, the sixth of October, we stayed over in Arcos, sketching, photographing and admiring the town.

There was so much to see. To an architect, I imagine, a great deal more than much, to an archeologist an endless source of interest. To any artist the whole city is a visual treat. I hardly saw Greg; he was busy shooting all day long.

Three churches spreading along the ridge in this order, Santa Maria, San Pedro and San Martin, are of special interest. They are beautiful Gothic examples, all three, but Santa Maria dominates the town. Topped only by the castle itself, the flying buttresses of this great church span houses, markets and narrow streets, like a great bird holding the town in its talons. In a large part of the city one is always looking up at them soaring overhead.

A convent of a slightly later date, the Covento de Monjas de la Mercedería, once began to add on next to it a large eighteenth-century chapel. It was very elegant with a beautifully columned portico, but beyond the first level the money ran out. They sold it to the city which made out of it the most charming and elegant open-air market, with mat screens against the sun painting a lovely pattern back and forth over the colorful stalls; certainly the most gracious market place one could imagine.

We were lucky in the moon that night, and so Arcos gave us a spectacular good-by. We wandered for a while through the streets

33

and on the battlements, but morning was coming soon and a long trail lay ahead to Algar on the frontier of the province of Cádiz.

The next day found us gingerly picking our way down the switchback streets from the top of the cliffs to the Rio Guadalete, running placidly between poplar trees in the meadows far below. From the the river the fantastic city above looked as if it were moving through the clouds behind it. Across the river a new type of terrain lay before us.

All through our journey we were being surprised by these sudden changes in landscape. If we had wanted to we could have ridden in the space of one hour from yesterday's wild mountain pass, truly stark, through the city, across placid river meadows a thousand feet below, and now, cliffs at our back, we faced a seemingly limitless expanse of gently rising olive groves dotted with big and little ranch houses.

The horses, moving lightly, feeling their day of rest, carried us quickly over the dark red earth that is typical of the land where olives grow. The only earth of this same rich red that I have seen is in the sugar-cane fields of Hawaii. These groves continued for three or four hours, finally thinning out into pine forests. We passed two or three horsemen, but there seemed to be no inhabitants of any sort until we came to a place where the pine trees had been pruned of their lower branches, a sure sign that we were coming into an area of the charcoal burners.

The charcoal burners of Spain are a very important part of the life of the peninsula, for charcoal, especially in the country districts, serves both for cooking and heating. It is the main source of fuel. The *carboneros* lead a strange and nomadic life. With no fixed home, a tiny group of families will move through the forests, putting up their lean-to huts, clipping at the pine trees as high as is practicable, forming their great charcoal pits, and then moving on when an area has been exhausted. Men, women and children,

34

all black as the ace of spades from constant exposure to their trade, they move clannishly and secretively through all the high forests of Spain.

On the wildest mountain trails we would come upon a long string of their charcoal-laden burros delivering their loads to the nearest trucking station, then with a few supplies disappearing again into the dark forests.

We were in high country again, crossing the Sierra de Vallejo; ahead lay three mountain ranges progressively higher and wider between us and Ronda, dominated by the enormous rose-colored peak of Grazalema, still two days' ride away.

It was a cool, pleasant and largely uneventful day. By about three o'clock we came to a tiny country store at the crossing of another trail. We stopped for a while, had a beer and rested the horses. All through the ride we found we made our best time by not stopping seriously at midday. Rather we took a late start about nine o'clock, which gave Greg the morning light to take photographs of whatever town we stayed in. Then we would ride if possible only until about five o'clock so that he would have an afternoon light for more photography. This October the seventh we came by half past six to Argal, lying along a ridge among pine trees and eucalyptus. It was a sleepy little mountain town of no importance or antiquity with one long cobbled main street. On either side the gentlemen of Argal, sitting at coffee tables on the tiny sidewalk, bowed polite welcome, murmured a dignified salutation; three blocks ahead was our goal, the Posada de San Diego.

The streets of Argal, like most mountain villages, had a center gutter with a corresponding slope, so you can see that each cross street formed a saucer. Along we came, skidding and sliding, trying to preserve our dignity and *sang-froid*. Burgo led with one pack horse; I followed, then Antonio with two pack horses head to tail; Greg brought up the rear.

36

At the *posada* Burgo dismounted and led in. I dismounted, started in, and then it happened! Behind me I heard a tremendous clatter of hoofs. I let Bejeriegos loose and turned just in time to see three horses down. Antonio's horse had slipped and fallen on him in the saucer; one pack horse had gone over them, and the other pack horse had fallen into a café table! Greg was dismounted and pulling Banderas off Antonio; the members of the corner café gang had Antonio sitting in a chair—all this by the time I had covered the twenty yards back to them! It seemed that nothing had broken against the big cobbles. Antonio, in considerable pain, was carried, chair and all, into the *posada*. We got Antonio's foot into a bucket of cold water, stalled the horses and sent for the village doctor. By this time the whole town was around. Praises were raised. Good luck, *señores! Mala fortuna, amigos!* But the horses were fine, nothing hurt. Hell! I thought, how bad is the damage? We were soon to find out.

The *posada* at Argal was typical, so I'll describe it. You ride the animals in the big street door and right through a huge room, the main room of the inn, opening into a central courtyard with a well and drinking trough in the middle. Stabling is all around the other three sides. The main room or *comedor* is flagstone-floored like the courtyard. A huge hooded fireplace fills the whole far end from wall to wall. No windows, only the great door to the street and the open archway to the courtyard. Along the walls thick iron pegs are set in, hung with saddles and bridles, sacks and saddlebags, the varied belongings of the patrons; standing against the wall two rows of rush-bottomed chairs, a long refectory table down the middle. Across from the fireplace is a well-worn stone stairway with no handrail leads to the sleeping rooms above, each with wash-hand stand, iron bed and chair. In the courtyard, two outside privies. On the hearth the innkeeper's family are preparing dinner. This is the usual picture.

By the time we had settled in and bedded and fed the animals, I had the first-aid kit out and had put a loose bandage on Antonio's foot and ankle, which were badly swollen. The doctor was out of town and not expected until later in the evening, so we pulled up chairs to the big table and settled down to a typical country dinner. The food was simple but very good: soup, *fabadas,* a partridge and a *cocido,* or stew. With it they had a rough red wine and sent to the corner for beers. Dessert was apples. This was typical of the meals we were to enjoy. And the cost of it—room, dinner and breakfast—was sixty pesetas, or a dollar a head. Grain and stabling for the horses came out at thirty, so that for a dollar and a half a day a man can live pretty comfortably in the mountains of Spain. Double that for all incidentals, and life resolves itself for under a hundred dollars a month and some of the most beautiful scenery in the world thrown in free.

About nine o'clock the young doctor turned up on his Vespa. After a thorough examination he diagnosed Antonio's foot as being badly sprained and strapped and bandaged it. This was bad news.

I wanted to send the boy back to Jerez in a local Land Rover and have it bring back a replacement for him; but Antonio's disappointment was so keen and his desire to finish the trip with us so great that I finally gave in to his pleas. We decided to lay over for the day of the eighth, give him a good rest, and see how the foot did.

The following morning Antonio felt a bit better, although there was no question of getting a boot on his foot. Still he had all day to keep off it, so, leaving him fairly comfortable, Greg and I set off to find out what we could about Argal.

The town, although it has an ancient look, is only a bit over two hundred years old. It was then that the Marqués de Carvajal, voyaging home from the Indies, was caught in a great storm. As the ship seemed about to be overwhelmed he vowed to the Virgen de

Guadalupe that if he was saved he would build to Her Glory, in the spot in his own province of Cádiz most remote from the sea, a church and a town. Here in the high mountains on the border of the province he found his site.

Bringing ninety families, he established Argal. Where a stream of good size gushes from the mountain he ordered his architect to build a mill. The architect demurred at the expense of building at that spot, but the Marqués placed ten *onzas* of gold from the Indies at the corner of the proposed site. Naturally convinced by this lavish gesture, the architect bowed, the mill was built, and the town has prospered from it to this day. This little millstream is now the source of the main water supply of Jerez so far away.

The following morning Antonio's foot was down a lot. Though he still could not get a boot on, he begged to continue. The next automobile road we would contact was ten hours' hard ride away; I had my misgivings. But the boy insisted, we hadn't the heart to refuse him. We padded his saddle with a rolled-up blanket under his knee to ease the injured foot and at first dawn set out on our journey.

Ten hours in the saddle is always tough; over a pass a mile high with one water spot it is tougher. But beyond the Sierra del Pinar lay Grazalema, Antonio's home town, and he was determined he would make it. We could not favor him further; it was push, push all day or not at all.

Most of the morning was fairly easy, going up hill along the shoulder of a big mountain and then slowly down and through the *ganadaria* or bull-range of the Gonsález. From the thickets the young fighting-bulls, living, as is most proper, under wild conditions, watched our little train go by; in this ambiance they are quiet if not disturbed and a great pleasure to observe. Riding through the little herds of Toros Bravos in their natural habitat, watching them eye you speculatively as you whistle gently to quiet them, is an

41

exciting and rewarding experience. There is quite a difference between seeing bulls two and three years old a few feet away from your stirrup and watching them from the safety of a *barrera* seat.

Washington Irving obviously enjoyed the same thrill, for he says:

"Sometimes, in winding through the narrow valleys, he is startled by a hoarse bellowing, and beholds above him on some green fold of the mountain a herd of Andalusian bulls, destined for the combat of the arena. I have felt, if I may so express it, an agreeable horror in thus contemplating, near at hand, these terrific animals, clothed with tremendous strength, and ranging their native pastures in untamed wildness, strangers almost to the face of man; they know no one but the solitary herdsman who attends them, and even he at times dares not venture to approach them. The low bellowing of these bulls and their menacing aspect as they look down from their rocky height give additional wildness to the savage scenery."

At the other end of the valley of the bulls we jogged through some salt pans where the foreman, joining us, rode on a way and put us onto a short cut to a little mountain village, El Bosque. This was our watering point. Arriving at noon, we watered and rested the horses for half an hour, had a beer and pushed on. I had looked at Antonio's foot. It was definitely swelling, but we had passed our halfway mark and nothing remained but to get it over with.

From here on it got tougher; flinty trails led to harder and steeper rough, rocky climbs. Higher up it became a bit of a scramble. Antonio still smiled bravely, though he admitted the foot *picarse*, hurt itself.

At last, about four o'clock, the worst was over. Riding very high along the side of the huge rose-colored mountain of Grazalema, we hit a flint-paved mountain road that led through the top of the pass.

From where we were the valley fell steeply down at one side,

the enormous cliffs towered overhead. Far below a little river watered groves of trees and a few cultivated fields. Halfway up the far slope of this great valley, on a little tableland, stood a ranch house in a grove of trees. Through the glasses we could see activity around its corrals and from time to time we could hear shotguns, though no hunters were in sight. This country is thick with partridges, the big Spanish *perdiz,* wonderful shooting and very fine eating. As I slipped the glasses back into the case, I thought what a wonderful place to own!

By five o'clock we breasted the pass and started down a long series of switchbacks to where, halfway down the mountain, lay Grazalema. Antonio was home!

On the outskirts, the minute we arrived at those treacherous cobbled skidways, I ordered a dismount. No more grand entries, *amigos;* one casualty was enough. Leading our horses and helping poor Antonio, who could bare hobble, we made our way through town to the *posada.*

The first stop for Antonio was the *médico,* who took one look, rebandaged the foot, gave Antonio a shot of painkiller and announced the expected verdict. Then and there I chartered a car and off he went to the clinic at Ronda and the x-ray machine, to be laid up until we arrived two days later. As we intended to be in Ronda a couple of days it would give him four days' rest. However, I was pretty sure the trip was over for him.

This day we had one of the hardest rides I have ever made. We had climbed five thousand feet, crossed two mountain ranges and been in the saddle with only one dismount for practically twelve hours. Only Burgo, the iron man, was untired. You may be sure that we slept well that night.

Seldom has a town been placed in a more dramatic setting than Grazalema; right in the throat of the pass the great rocky peaks literally tower over it on three sides up to an unbelievably blue

44

cloudless sky. Below, the slopes fell away and away down to the wide *vega* across which, enthroned on its tableland a day's ride distant, Ronda rules all the country around her.

Grazalema is an old, very old, and beautiful city which has probably guarded this pass since time immemorial, but oddly enough, it has no history at all.

During the civil war all records, the city archives were destroyed by the Rojos, and the local historian, it appears, died last year, leaving no notes. The citizens simply do not know, have scant recollection of more than fifty years back! It is frustrating, for this town must be full of history. Architecturally one can see that it was Iberian, Roman, Spanish, Arabic, for all these cultures have left their traces. In the main square a Roman fountain which served as our watering trough was fed from spouts of copper sunk into the mouths of four prehistoric Iberian heads! Castles and fortifications in various conditions of ruin abound; in the plaza stands a church with a beautiful Romanesque façade which has obviously been destroyed once up to the façade and rebuilt behind it later. Its foundations are Roman. By whom destroyed? When? By whom rebuilt? ¿Quien sabé? Who knows?

There is a sort of an hermitage on the mountain above the town. Once, they say, it was occupied by monks, but they were discourteous to travelers and gave no aid, so eventually were driven out. Who were they? Who drove them out? When? No one remembers.

During our day in Grazalema, the tenth of October, Greg was busy all over town taking photos. Burgo was having the horses' shoes reset after yesterday's hard scramble over the rocky trail. I spent the day with the Mayor, a very intelligent young man of about thirty, trying to puzzle out some answers to the many questions this lovely town presented. It was no use.

The main industry is weaving. This is the local center of the

46

wool industry, and from here come most of the beautiful and practical ponchos that are worn by all the vaqueros, shepherds and farmers throughout these mountains. They are dyed in blue, a deep crimson lake, bleached white, and some left a natural tan color. Piped in contrasting colors and tasseled at the neck and at the corners, these are most handsome garments. Thrown over the head, they hang to below the knee, and as the natural oil is left in the wool, they are not only wonderfully warm but absolutely waterproof. I bought seven of these fine garments, used one myself for the rest of the journey and gave others to skiers among my friends and family. They have all used them, loved them and think that if these products were ever exported from their mountain home they would have a big vogue—but I suppose they will simply go on making enough to fill the local demand, and only travelers to this far-off place will enjoy their warm protection.

According to the Mayor, three years ago a French moving-picture company came to Grazalema and made a movie, hiring a great many of the citizens to work in it. Ever since then the town has been populated by frustrated actors who sit around in the sun waiting for another cinema company to come and employ them. They have never seen the picture, for Grazalema naturally has no theatre, but their hopes flourish in spite of it. In fact they lost all interest in us when they found we weren't an advance party for a future production.

From Grazalema to Ronda is only about a six-hour ride, so the following morning, having hired a vaquero, Benítez, a frustrated actor, to take Antonio's place, we set off for one of the easiest, most pleasant stages of our ride.

The trail to Ronda, after the first few miles down the grassy mountain slopes, led through pleasant groves of pine and oak trees, across wide grasslands and through ranches and the tiny villages that hem that fabulous city.

Asking our way as we went, we came with no trouble at all to the foot of the high mesa, cleft by a gorge, on which Ronda stands. As we came to the trail leading upward we were stopped by two Guardia Civil, who came scrambling down a hillside to look over our papers. While Burgo produced all these, for a pack train, like a ship, must carry bills of lading and identification when traveling through the provinces, Greg started taking snapshots of the two officials in their Napoleonic hats from where he sat in his saddle.

Mind you, these two men were only doing their duty, and most courteously at that, but I immediately sensed a feeling of truculence on the part of my vaqueros. It was unreasonable but typical of the arrogant Spanish attitude of independence and of impatience with authority.

My God, I thought, the pride, the overweening, misdirected pride of these passionate people! A simple thing like being asked to show a *permiso* is, to them, an immediate infringement of their rights, their personality; no wonder these men are hard to rule and almost impossible to command!

Once a good friend of mine, a Duque who shall be nameless, explained, "We need a King, Jaime. Believe me we must always have someone, some institution, above politics and politicians, for no Spaniard can feel at ease being ruled by his equal. Why? Because we are all anarchists at heart.

"I am an anarchist, I confess it; so is my bootblack, my chauffeur, my tailor, most of my friends. To be a Spaniard is to be by nature anarchistic.

"Above all, Jaime, a Spaniard is an individual. His preoccupation is in himself first of all, then, in order, in his family, his town and finally his province—beyond that who cares? *¿Quien se preocupa?*"

Of course my good friend was probably exaggerating a great

deal. After all, a country that has managed to build up its economy at the fantastic rate that Spain has in the last ten years, a country that has managed to control the inflation which is troubling the rest of Europe and at the same time not only develop a huge tourist business but also attract millions and millions of foreign capital, must assuredly have a certain degree of co-operation. However, the Spaniard is without doubt the world's greatest individualist; only supreme egoists could have conquered the Americas with a few hundred determined men.

While one of the Guardia was mulling through the papers the other looked up and caught Greg busy with his camera. At once we were in trouble! The Guardia explained that it was strictly against the law to take photographs of members of that elite organization. They now wanted to confiscate the whole roll of film. Although I try never to argue with authority, I decided it was time I swung my age, so I stepped in and explained, passing around cigarettes, that the young señor was a *fotografo* very serious and highly regarded in the United States, a devoted friend of Spain, who had only wished to preserve a picture of such estimable members of their proud Corps for a record which would be viewed all over the world. Also a lie, that there were a hundred pictures on this roll, the record of days of voyaging, which would be lost if exposed. Greg in his beautiful Spanish assured them that he had no intention of offending such reasonable gentlemen and that he would not, on his word of honor, publish the picture. Politeness prevailed, and with mutual regard we left them and commenced the pleasant climb up a shady path which led us out on the top of the tableland almost exactly at the gate of our hotel.

Here in Ronda stands the Reina Victoria on the very lip of the mesa, set in beautiful gardens, one of the most comfortable and certainly most dramatically situated hotels in Spain. Here no *posada,* but hot baths and all the comforts.

As we rode into the hotel courtyard the first thing we saw was Greg's beautiful bronze Jaguar, so we knew that Suzy, his charming wife, had driven up from Marbella to meet us. While Greg went in to fetch her, I unloaded the saddlebags and sent Burgo, Benítez and one of the bellboys off with the horses to the *posada,* only three blocks away, where I told Burgo I would meet him with a car in half an hour to go to the clinic and get The Word on Antonio.

Meeting Suzy, checking in, sending out our laundry and having a beer took no time at all, then we picked up Burgo and drove to the hospital. All the news was bad. The doctor took us in to where Antonio was propped up in bed with a cast over his ankle and an x-ray showing three bones in his foot badly broken. There was no question now of the poor boy finishing the trip.

I went back to the *posada* with Burgo and looked over the pack horses. Two of them had badly galled backs from those hard mountain rides. We talked it over and decided to send a truck back to Jerez with them and Antonio. It would be a five-hour drive where we had taken six days. The truck could bring back two mules to take their place, as Burgo thought the mules would serve us better in the mountains that lay ahead.

That night I got on the phone to Delgado in Jerez. He said it would take a day to get the proper mules, so we arranged for the truck to go down on October 13, a Sunday, and come back that afternon with the fresh animals. In the meantime Benítez, delighted to go on to Granada, which he had never seen, telegraphed his family in Grazalema to send him up some clothing by bus. We settled down to wait.

If one has to possess one's soul in patience, I must say there can be no better place in the world to do it in than the fabulous city of Ronda. So many guidebooks have been written, so many paintings and photographs have been made, so many stories told of this unique city, that I am not going to try to add much to them.

For the next two days we lazied around—I did, not Greg—enjoying its wonderful sights, its beautiful palaces strung along the cliffs overlooking the ruins of the Roman baths below. Many of the great Andalucian families had summer palaces here. Some of them still are occupied, some empty but on view, two are museums, two antique shops.

Everywhere you wander through its streets and plazas you see new beauties, new lovely vistas.

A narrow gorge like a sword cut slashes straight through the town and the mesa on which it stands, dividing it into what are now referred to as the Spanish and Arab towns. Across this chasm, hundreds of feet deep, the Romans threw a fantastic bridge, for the whole town was once one of the chief Roman cities in Spain. Inside the arches of this bridge, between the top of the arch and the roadway above, is a club-restaurant from the windows of which you can see the eagles flying up the gorge beneath you.

It is a strange thing about Ronda. Everyone already seems to know about this city. Even people who have never seen it know that of all the world's towns this is perhaps the most glamorously situated, and yet there is no outstanding architectural monument in it. Sacheverell Sitwell, a great authority on art and architecture, loves this town dearly but can only give one or two pages to it; after describing the bull ring he says the same thing that occurs to me: "Ronda is . . . Ronda, and the eagles are always soaring beneath the level of the cliffs." What more can I say?

I am no romantic, I hope, but what can you say of a city where you look out of any window and watch the eagles coasting by.

Ronda is full of beautiful houses, even some palaces, many of which I have enjoyed, but how can I, no architect, no *cognosciento* of periods or of detail, describe what Sitwell leaves undetailed.

As I said before, the deep cleft, the *tajo*, that slices through the town divides the southern or Moorish part from the newer district

53

to the north. The contrast between the two towns is extreme and interesting. There are three buildings in the old town that I think are of special interest because they are all additions to ancient edifices. The first, the Minarete Arabe, is now the Christian church of San Sebastían, really a reconstruction of the ancient Mezquita or Mosque. Another is the church of Santa María la Mayor; this beautiful church was built in 1485 on the remains of a temple dedicated to Julius Caesar. And the third, which really carries you back in time, is the Colegio Salesiano, erected on the remains of the old Castle of the Laurel. Here let the student of history walk reverently, for this was built by the Greeks.

On another corner of the ruins of this great Attic fortress the Moors built the Tower of Ochavada. This was not allowed to rest in peace, however, for on top of it again is the Gothic church of Espíritu Santu; builders in those days certainly did not lack for inspiring foundations. While on the subject of ancient buildings, although we were staying at the hotel our men and horses were housed in the Posada de las Animas. This dates back to 1500 and we were far from its most important patrons, for Miguel de Cervantes, the author of *Don Quixote,* lived there for a year.

A church of great interest, founded by Ferdinand and Isabella, is the Iglesia de la Virgen de Gracia. Not very large, of late-Gothic style, it belongs not to the Church but to the Royal Maestranza de Caballería de Ronda, who also built and owns the beautiful bull ring, the oldest *Plaza de Toros* in Spain.

This city is a mood, a group of fine furniture makers, a small band of great saddlers, a few dramatic mountain friends who seem a bit different from other men because they are Rondeños. An alpine air, a feel of falcons, an old man I know seen galloping up a back street just after doing me a great favor.

God knows, you could pack craftsmen, sportsmen and businessmen together in four walls on the top of a mesa, but they aren't

54

Rondeños. Only in this city with eagles at their feet do the men become the city, more than the city makes the man. These mountaineers make the town they live in. From the first Roman to Antonio Ordoñez this is true.

How can you live constantly with eagles below you without being a bit different from other men?

So all I can say of Ronda is that each moment spent there is an exciting hour.

Don Miguel Puya Gonzáles and his wife are so typical.

In Andalucía one comes to expect endless hospitality, an interest in your problems and your needs far beyond normal. If you live in Andalucía you take as your right what would normally be impositions; you're badly spoiled.

Suddenly you find yourself surrounded by friends who extend themselves beyond belief. You don't know why, but you ride into town and find your money is no good. I don't mean in the hotel bar, but in other ways. One night an old saddler arrived at the hotel carrying a real work of art on his shoulder, saying:

"It was said, señor, that the saddle you are riding is not exactly the type of *montera* that we pride ourselves on here in the hills, so I have one for you to take with you on your way." From who? Nobody? Somebody?

I found out later it was Miguel Puya. "After all, Jimmy," he explained, "one must see that one's friends are as comfortably seated as possible." From there to Granada I was.

Of course, to the *aficionado* Ronda is the capital of Spain. For it is the home of Romero, the first of the great bullfighters on foot, the man who invented the passes and the conventions by which bulls are fought today. In the central park his statue stands facing the Plaza de Toros. This bull ring is architecturally far the most beautiful in existence and at this time was being very carefully and conscientiously restored, as too many of us had taken

55

falls down its crumbling old stone steps. The restoration is being done under the watchful eye of this dear friend of mine, Don Miguel Puya Gonzáles, one of Ronda's leading citizens, who assured me that it would be impossible to tell where the necessary work began and the antique ended.

Every year in August one of the finest *corridas* in Spain is held here in memory of Pedro Romero. It is always fought in "Goyesca"; in other words, the *toreros,* the bull-ring servants, everyone involved, are in the costume of the period of Goya, the time when Romero lived.

To add to the brilliance of the spectacle several of the great bull breeders send up their six-horse teams of beautifully matched horses who perform the most intricate feats of driving in the bull ring before the fights. The Osbornés of Jerez have a team of matched greys, six horses with a canterer, a horse galloping completely loose in front, controlled by word of mouth from the coachman, through figure eights and the most complicated patterns, he being unbridled and free. This is one of the most unusual exhibitions of driving one can see anywhere.

To add to this, the three leading *toreros* of the year, if possible, take part in this *corrida* for which the six best *ganadarías* of Andalucía each hold back and present what they consider to be their finest bull, for which a prize is given. The resulting spectacle can be imagined.

As the ring is small the tickets are hard to come by and most are held from year to year; I never miss it. Each August finds me in the string of cars going up that wild mountain road with its five hundred curves in fifty kilometers, and I am always amply rewarded for the terrors of the trip!

Well do I remember a fight seven years ago when the great Antonio Ordoñez, himself a Rondeño, met the perfect bull at Ronda.

This greatest of *toreros,* then at his peak, saw after the first few passes that he was facing one of those animals that, carefully handled and lovingly developed, could produce the ultimate performance for which *aficionados* pray. This beautiful beast, majestically horned, full of fire, intelligent and fierce, was a supreme product of the famous *ganadaría* of the Guardiola family of Sevilla.

Antonio, in a beautiful series of linked *verónicas*, presented it for the picador. The bull charged with great fierceness, and the picador, placing his *palo* perfectly, exactly in the great swelling *moro* of the bull's shoulder, circled his horse carefully on the bull until the *torero* made the *quité*, drawing the bull out into the ring. Then in a series of passes in the slow, classical Rondeño style that has given its name to this school of fighting, he proceeded to bring the audience to its feet. By now the maestro, realizing what a jewel he had facing him, petitioned the judges that the *suerte* of the *varas*, the pics, should end. The judges, Alvaro

Domecq, Juan Belmonte and El Gallo, agreed. So with only the single pic the fight moved into the *suerte* of the *banderillas*.

Anxious that the *toro* should come to him in the last stages of the fight unhurt, in its full power, with its magnificent courage unimpaired, Ordóñez allowed only one pair of *banderillas* to be placed. As he walked to the *barrera* to take his sword and muleta for this last and great stage of the fight, the crowd had literally gone mad with enthusiasm.

To see a bull of this quality fought with only one pic and one pair was rare, "una barbaridad!"

Adding to the mounting emotion, the great *espada* now walked slowly along the *barrera* and stopped in front of his father, the great retired matador Niño de la Palma. To him he dedicated this living legend of a bull. At this point enthusiasm was so high that tears mingled with the wild cheering of the plaza.

The *faena* which followed was so beautiful and so complete that it is impossible to praise it too much.

Antonio developed his *faena* with absolutely perfect passes of every category; so slow, so sure, so close was he working that the pair, man and beast, looked like a living group of statuary. As one pass melted into the next perfect pass the maestro kept building confidence and glory in the bull; the animal, responding, kept adding to the luster of the man.

The entire audience was spellbound by this time; even the cheering had subsided to automatic *"Olés,"* like great sighs, after each pass; the entire crowd had succumbed to Antonio's magic and was experiencing the fight with him. It was impossible to explain this tremendous rapport! It seemed incredible that the tension could be prolonged another moment, yet pass after pass it continued, the two performers like two tireless dancers in love!

For the glorious finale of this magnificent performance Antonio Ordóñez, in the middle of the plaza, planted like a tree, killed

*recibiendo* with one sure thrust. In other words, he received the full charge without moving his feet and the bull dropped dead in front of him, a method rarely seen in these effete days. Juan Belmonte said to me, "Jimmy, always remember this, for this is the greatest *faena* I have ever seen."

The crowd had become hysterical. The presidents awarded him both ears, the tail and the hoof and ordered the dead bull to be given a *vuelta,* or a circle of the plaza, the greatest of honors. As Antonio, to the frantic cheering, took his *vuelta* walking beside the bull, he kept shaking one hand negatively at the ecstatic crowd and pointing with his other hand at the great dead beast, indicating, "Not to me, gentlemen, to the animal the glory." It was without doubt the most gracious gesture and the most emotional moment I have ever experienced in watching the killing of over a thousand bulls.

To return from the sublime to the ridiculous. The mules turned up on Sunday night—unshod! So instead of an early departure on Monday that day had to be devoted to getting them ready for the many rocky kilometers that lay ahead. Even beautiful Ronda had begun to pall, and in spite of the limitless hospitality of Don Miguel Puya and his delightful wife we were becoming impatient to be riding again.

However, Thursday saw us on our way to Candéte Reál, an easy six-hour ride. The voyage was uneventful through rolling farmlands, gradually climbing in the afternoon, a good *camino vaquero* under foot, a drover's road skirting the mountains all the way to this delightful town.

Candéte, on the foothills of the high Sierras, was once the seat of the Duques de la Molina. Although the family has died out or at least left long ago, we came into the town past the ornate façade of their family palace and also houses of the Duques de Alba and of Alcalá. We were impressed by the elegance of these buildings

beautifully decorated with heraldic blazons over their porticos. This was evidently a solid and substantial town for many generations past.

We rode into a large and gracious central plaza with two or three good cafés, the *ayuntamiento,* or city hall, and a church on three sides, and the *posada* on the fourth.

We found the *posada* had stabling but only one unoccupied bedroom. However, giving the bedroom to our vaqueros, we found very comfortable quarters in a small inn nearby.

As we walked across the square carrying our saddlebags we found it full of groups of men smoking, talking, sitting in the cafés, but, as is usual in these mountain cities, no women.

In these old-fashioned towns a woman's place is very definitely in the home. The custom of the *Paseo* where the young ladies in groups stroll in the plaza in the evening to be admired doesn't hold true here. You never see women in cafés; in fact you have the feeling you are living in a large men's club. The fair sex venture out marketing or on errands but otherwise seem strictly kept at home. In their houses you dine with the men, the women serve. Of course this probably isn't true at times of *feria* or fiesta, but we found it pretty habitual all through the mountains. I must say it robs the towns of glamour.

We were impressed with the quality of Candéte. Many of the houses, some almost palaces, had fine decorated façades emblazoned with coats of arms. The whole had a degree of elegance. On the hill above it is a large Roman fort, partly in ruins, with Arab superstructure. Greg planned to spend a lot of time with his camera up there in the morning. Most of the ranches around were big and prosperous. Winter wheat had been planted, and good-looking herds of beef cattle and pigs were to be seen grazing.

In our little inn the hostess cooked our dinner over an open fire on the kitchen floor. A rich soup with vermicelli, roast partridge,

62

an omelet and a fine melon, local wine and good black coffee. Room and board cost a dollar and a half a day.

After dinner we walked out into the central plaza for another coffee and found it still more crowded, partly with townspeople, but about half were by their dress obviously farmers and ranchers of the neighborhood.

The square is dominated by a tall statue, electrically lighted, of the Virgen de las Canas. People that we chatted with all kept pointing her out. They seemed very proud because this *Virgen* is particular to the town. I couldn't figure out just what this meant, but apparently she is a miraculous *Virgen* and in some way connected with the city water supply. It was all rather vague. This statue is of great antiquity but lit up with electric lights like a Christmas tree.

We both had very comfortable rooms with good soft beds but of course no plumbing; as usual, the outhouse was in the patio. However, I slept very well until awakened in the morning by the unmistakable scent of frying *churros* in the street outside.

I got up and looked out of the window, and sure enough, across the narrow lane against the wall of the church a *churrero* had set up his stand. Over his brazier was a great pot of boiling oil and in it he was frying, like doughnuts, the wonderful pretzel-shaped crisp bread sticks that make the finest accompaniment to morning coffee.

I pulled on my clothes and boots over the long underwear in which we always slept (no pajamas on this trip), went down the corridor and wakened Greg, then, muffled against the nippy morning in my quilted jacket, went out and stood in line with the early housewives at the *churros* stand. By the time Greg had joined me I was at the head of the line and collecting a dozen of these piping hot delicacies in a cone of newspaper. We took them up to the corner café and sat down before two big glasses of *café con leche*. There is a story about Alfonso XIII, then in exile in Italy, who when

63

asked by a well-meaning visitor what Spanish thing he most missed, answered *"Churros, hombre."* Anyone who has enjoyed them can understand the poor king's sentiment.

After breakfast Greg, loaded with cameras, took off for his scramble up the mountain to the castle ruins. By the time he had disappeared, a tiny figure under its imposing walls, the sun was well up and I set out in search of the secretary of the city government, Don Inocencio Ruíz Martín, to whom Miguel Puya had given me a letter of introduction.

This courteous and helpful gentleman I found in the Office of Archives of the city hall. Passing through two courtyards of a delightful old palace, mounting to the colonnaded *galería* of the second floor, I was led into a long well-lighted room in which three or four gentlemen were working at antique stand-up desks. One entire wall was bookshelves containing, besides volumes both old and antique, ancient folders bound around and around with crumbling ribbons of varicolored silks, the colors of the families of the town. These folders held loosely not only the archives and records but contracts, private letters, bills of sale, negotiations of property and various legal papers; in fact the entire paper work of Candéte goes back to 1537. What a contrast to the destroyed archives of the unfortunate Grazalema!

With obvious and appropriate pride Don Inocencio and his clerks began spreading all this treasure before me. It was too much! There was material here for months of fascinating research had I the time. It was very hard, as a matter of fact, to explain to this helpful dignitary that I had not arrived inspired by the thought of compiling a history of his town; so I satisfied myself with going through the papers of the Duques of Alba, which were tremendously interesting and showed that the Spanish nobles, unlike most' of the Italians, had acquired their lands not by conquest but by royal grant or largely by purchase. Deeds, bills of sale, contracts and

64

receipts made up the greater part of these permanent records.

Knowing that Greg would be equally fascinated by this historical treasure trove, I promised to return with him after lunch. On the way out Don Inocencio pointed out the motto on the arms of the city: "We had commercial importance among the Phoenicians." I walked through the sunlit patio under the shadow of the *entrada* and out into the street. I looked at my watch; it suddenly seemed silly strapped there on my wrist . . . "the time of the Phoenicians . . ." How irrelevant time had become.

This was midmorning; the town by now was naturally about its daily business, active, but with no sense of impelling immediacy. I strolled toward the plaza happily, conscious that all around me was an atmosphere of quiet purpose, not urgency. Secluded on its mountainside, Candéte Reál was going about its daily tasks exactly as it had, year in, year out, season following season, since it had "commercial importance" in the time of that vanished race.

At a table in the plaza I ordered a *café solo* and settled down to wait for Greg, who I knew was athletically and photographically involved up the mountainside in the ruins of the fort. Before me gradually unfolded the most pleasant, yet busy urban scene one could imagine. Across the square a train of burros loaded with building tiles daintily followed their leader; as is usual in Spain, he answered the shouted voice of command of the *arriero,* the muleteer, who walked at the tail of the procession. It was interesting to see the whole line, at his call, stop to let a loaded beer truck pass by their noses and draw up at my café, then go on again and at his signal turn leftward up the hill toward their destination. Under the arcade of the Ayuntamiento two policemen gravely saluted a group of ladies on their way to market, each with a shopping bag on her arm and, as always, a plate for meat or fish in the other hand.

In front of the café opposite two important-looking men climbed out of a Land Rover, to be effusively welcomed by an equally im-

65

portant trio obviously intent on "*negocios*", business of great serious-ness. Now occurred one of those anomalies so often seen in this mysterious land. Around the corner of the church rode an old and ragged *caballero,* gaunt and tall, a picture of Don Quixote, on an equally tall and starveling roan gelding. Immediately the group around the Land Rover stiffened to attention. Those who had hats on swept them off; the others bowed. The old gentleman, nodding courteously, rode off across the square. Who was he? You could see, as they knew, *muy hidalgo,* great gentry. Thank God there is one land on earth where personality, not Land Rovers, commands respect.

To the right, in front of the *posada,* I saw my two vaqueros sunning themselves and making lazy and licentious approaches to the market girls who had set up their stalls along its front. A man walked by skillfully wheeling a heavy T beam on his bicycle; three farmers dismounted from their mules, took the table next to me and began busily discussing the crops. The town was active, busy but not too busy, and it seemed to me that here in Candéte people had arrived at life's ideal tempo.

This little city, I thought to myself, untouched by impressive commerce, only blessed by dignity and elegance, must certainly be an enchanting place in which to live. Tossing down a couple of pesetas for my coffee, I crossed the plaza and walked on down the street by which we had entered the town, to have another look at the lovely houses that we had passed the day before. Seen at leisure, they were even more delightful, more enticing to the eye than at my first impression. Five or six of them, half palace, half mansion, were spaced along on either side of two or three blocks. Probably each one had originally stood in its own demesne, but the town had grown up around them. One, soft lavender in color and smaller than the others, was set a few yards back from the pave-ment behind the local conception of a Palladian frontal. A pair of

66

marble stairs led to the open doorway through which I could see a charming flowery patio. While I was admiring this rustic bijoux, an old lady came out with a bucket, a broom and a little sack of sand and began to scrub the steps.

Interrupting the old lady at her task, I asked her about the house. Only too pleased to stop her work, she said that if I was interested she would be glad to show me over the place as it had been long unoccupied. I followed her into the patio which was small but delightfully arranged with four old olive trees in the corners, criss-crossed by paths of marble chips converging on a very lovely small Mudejar fountain. Mudejar is the type of Spanish design that was developed in the sixteenth century and is a sort of bastard Moorish, slightly coarser and heavier, but still retaining an Arab elegance. Then she led me into the *sala,* high ceilinged, very simple décor, in fact enhanced only by very handsome frames on the tall street windows and the most gracious bolection molding around the fire-place on the opposite wall. The whole room was painted an arti-choke green with the moldings and detail picked out in a lighter shade of the same color. The floor was not of tile or marble but a very fine parquet, highly polished and dark with age, which showed the house to be, for Candéte, quite modern and perhaps not more than two hundred or so years old.

On the other side of the *entrada* or entrance hall which ran from the front door to the patio was a small salon opening onto the dining room; all these rooms forming the façade were totally un-furnished. On the other three sides around the patio were obviously kitchens, servants' rooms and so forth; upstairs I did not go. By this time I had found out that the place was the property of a young acquaintance, scion of one of the greatest families in Spain in whose houses in Salamanca and Madrid I had been entertained. From the servant I learned that the young man, who is one of Spain's most important hydraulic engineers, was the fourth generation of his family who had never seen the property, as she, her mother and her grandmother had all been housekeepers to landlords *in absentia*. This was not as shocking to me as it may sound to the reader, for the great Spanish families hold so much land and territories that in modern times you find that many of them have visited these investments no more often than one of us who might hold shares of U.S. Steel has visited Gary, Indiana. In fact, one of the most dramatic examples of this which I have run across is a tiny ruined keep guarding the long uncontested crossing of the Tormes River, far away in the Sierra de Gredos. This river crossing is called Puente de Alba, and from this ruined tower, now occupied by goats and chickens, that great family takes their name.

In these days when absentee landlord is an ugly name we must remember that land was once the only investment.

Wandering through these empty rooms, I gave my imagination free rein. Perhaps I am an escapist, but I couldn't help feeling how delightful it would be to live in this lovely little house, to furnish the deserted rooms, bring life into its waiting silence. When one reflects on the frenetic pace at which we live, how delicious to spend one's remaining years in the gentle ambiance of Candéte Réal.

Of course it was easy after so many days on the trail to overlook the absence of modern plumbing. As I remember from my childhood in Verona, a copper bathtub lined with a linen sheet really made for comfortable bathing, and a thoughtful man with a good library can always forego the cinema. Believe me, Candéte would offer far better compensations. I well remember Robert Benchley's recipe for a perfect day—one good meal, the exchange of one intelligent thought, one aesthetic experience, one good laugh, and so to bed with one good woman; at my age I don't know about the woman—one can only hope—but surely in these lovely surroundings the others would be most easily to hand. Who knows, with good shooting in the mountains, a good horse to ride, once a year London for the theater, Vienna for music—on four hundred dollars a month a man could be a king. . . . Don't push me too far, world!

I had managed in this pleasant manner to fritter away the remainder of the morning. Wandering back to the café and my rendezvous with Greg, I was greeted by a most delicious aroma. Following my nose, it led me to the kitchen where I found the *padrona* busily preparing a steaming *paella*. Somehow I hadn't expected to find this typical Andalúz dish so far from the sea; along the coast where I have my farm it is the traditional Sunday meal and, living on the Costa de Sol among a string of fishing villages, I had really forgotten that streams and rivers also yield fish and fresh-water shrimp.

In a big flat iron pan about two feet across steamed a bed of saffron rice; into this from a spicy marinade the good woman was spooning bits of white fish something like a mullet, small shrimps, gambi, and little river clams. To this she added shredded white meat of chicken and a bit of thinly sliced spicy *chorizo,* the tasty little mountain sausages; the only thing she lacked was *calamar,* the squid. This dish takes awhile to prepare, and by now I was absolutely ravenous, as you can imagine. Hesitantly I asked if there would be enough for us.

"But, señor"—she smiled—"this *paella* is all for you. El señor, your friend, the *caballero fotografo,* passed by half an hour ago and ordered this for you."

Mentally thanking Greg for his foresightedness, I settled back to wait for him and we were soon seated in front of this tasty dish flanked by a couple of bottles of delicious, ice-cold San Miguel beer.

By the time we had stowed all this away the place was putting up its shutters for the afternoon rest. There was nothing for it but to follow suit.

After a siesta Greg and I went back for another visit with Don

Inocencio Ruíz. We checked further on the history of the town and as usual found that after the Phoenicians came the ubiquitous Romans. In the usual course of history the empire falling gave way to the Gothic kings, who lost it eventually to the Moors. Over several hundred years they made Candéte into an important military post; restoring and strengthening the Roman fortifications and applying their usual scientific skills to the development of agriculture and the extension of a series of canals, they developed it into a quartermasters' depot and its influence in husbandry extended far beyond Campillos. They started, besides cattle and sheep, olives and great wheat farms which remain the principal commercial product of the area to this day.

Alfonso X in his reconquest bypassed the city until after the fall of Málaga; for this reason it escaped being taken by attack but was surrendered eventually to the Catholic kings when the Kingdom of Granada fell.

Greg had gotten all the photographs he wanted, so we decided to get an early start. As we were mounting in the morning, the cobblestones still slick with dew, my horse slipped and fell with me as I swung up. However, I stepped off as he went down and, barring a slightly wrenched knee, was all right. The horse was perfectly sound so, leading the nags, we headed out of town.

As we started across the plaza a very courteous old countryman, a total stranger to us, offered most kindly to walk along with us and put us on the mountain trail that, although hard to find, would lead us very pleasantly and by easy gradients down to the plain below. This innate helpfulness, this great Spanish courtesy, was typical of the treatment that we received at the hands of these wonderful people at every stage of our voyage. It was nothing at all to have a horseman or shepherd, on being asked a direction, to go a mile or more out of his way to be sure that we strangers were put on the best, the most convenient road.

The grace and dignity with which any Spaniard will put himself out to be of service is a natural characteristic. It is the sort of thing not often encountered in these days but a trait that seems to come as naturally as breathing to the inhabitants of the Peninsula.

This tradition of courtesy reminds me of the experience of a friend of mine in Madrid a couple of years ago. This lady, an American, was asked by some Spanish friends to go to the bull-fights with them one Sunday. She had never seen a fight, but having a very definite love of animals, a hatred of blood sports, in fact that ability of self-association with animals that in some people becomes almost a phobia, she very politely asked to be excused. However, this family, who were going to view the fight from their *palco,* or family box, way up at the very top of the stand, were gently insistent. From where they sat, they explained, one only saw the pageant as a whole, and they were sure she wouldn't be embarrassed by the sight of blood or any feeling of brutal contact. She let herself be persuaded but only on the condition that she would take along a book and if she felt at all disturbed would leave without interrupting their pleasure and sit out the rest of the *corrida* reading in the car.

Going into the ring, they were accosted by one of the professional beggars who work that beat. The Spaniards brushed him off as they entered, and soon everyone was comfortably settled in the *palco,* looking down on the miniature drama unfolding below.

My friend immensely enjoyed the *entrada* of the *cuadrillas* and the *toreros;* in fact she was very excited when the bull came in and she loved and appreciated the beautiful preliminary cape work. But the first time the bull went sock! into a horse she hastily got up, grabbed her book and, excusing herself, fled!

By the time she got to the car park she felt a little better, but when she found the car, to her despair, it was locked! This on top of her unnerving experience was too much for an already upset stomach, and she began to get hopelessly sick. Suddenly a shadow fell across her and, looking up, who should she see but the old beggar bowing gracefully in his rags and tatters.

"The señora is no doubt disturbed by the bulls?" With that he led her to a chair which he had borrowed from one of the candy sellers, brought her a glass of water, saw that she was comfortable, and when she tried to give him a hundred-peseta note, to him a windfall, smiled sweetly and said, "No, señora, I beg you . . . when I first encountered you I was simply plying my trade, but now I am only too glad to be of any little assistance," and with great dignity he walked away. Typical.

Today's ride was up a long valley and across rolling fields. Riding from ranch to ranch, sometimes through grazing lands, sometimes skirting great fields of wheat, we were seldom out of sight of plowmen, cattlemen, or shepherds. From them from time to time we asked our direction, always heading gradually to where out of sight beyond the horizon lay Campillos, our destination for the night. It was an uneventful but wonderfully pleasant, easy ride, a great contrast to the climbing of the last few days, for here we were on a vast high tableland.

In fact the only excitement of the day was when we came to a spot on a gentle hillside where our trail branched. From the lay of the land it looked as if one branch would eventually follow the main line of the valley while the other way, though seemingly a little better traveled, looked as if beyond our sight it might wander off into the hills. Which to take? Finally we saw someone near a well a quarter of a mile or so further down the hill. Riding down, we came on a spring which was spilling into a water trough. We stopped to water our horses, then rode down the brook a little further, and there was a woman kneeling on the bank washing clothes; an enormous straw hat covered her head and shoulders completely. Burgo called out a greeting; she straightened up, brushed back the great hat, and we found ourselves looking at one

of absolutely the most beautiful girls I have ever seen in my life.

Here I was, riding through the country of beautiful women, but loveliness, the sort I was staring at, caught you by the throat. I felt that dry-mouthed raspy feeling, that ache that goes from your throat through your chest down to the pit of your stomach and spreads.

It is funny, but I didn't think of her or where I was. Suddenly I went back through the years to an out-island far in the South Pacific where, years and years ago, I was sitting outside a Chinese trading store with Billy Fiske; Billy who was to become one of the falling embers that lit Biggin Hill when the Royal Air Force desperately won the Battle of Britain. When that light went out the aspirations of many a woman died with him. This enchanter, ugly as a mud fence, had the secret of each woman's heart. The sun was so hot it stung you through your shirt; suddenly a fifteen-year-old Bora Bora girl walked past us. She had the same beauty; she knew it, and we both looked at her, which added a swing to her hips. He said, "Jesus, she knows she's good looking, but she has no idea how beautiful she is. Do you ache too?" I did. Right now, in my old age, I ached the same; the difference between this girl and the girl from Bora Bora was that this one was completely unconscious of the sensation she caused.

She was so exquisite that we simply sat there in our saddles goggle-eyed, Greg fumbling madly in his saddlebags for his color camera. She was totally unaware of the excitement she was causing, utterly naïve and natural, reacting not a bit to Greg's frantic photography.

Burgo asked which was our proper road for Campillos. She did not know, so we tried her with a couple of names of villages en route closer at hand; the last one we knew was somewhere in the neighborhood, within at least an hour or two's ride. Finally she said, pointing to a farmhouse a hundred yards down the hill, "But,

74

señores, I have never been further than ten kilometers from that house."

We decided to take the lower road, so with her *"Vayan con Dios"* following us sweetly we dragged our reluctant photographer on our way. Two or three miles further on we found the other trail joining us again, so either would have done.

An hour's riding brought us to a railroad track. This we knew led us to Campillos, and sure enough, by three o'clock in the afternoon we saw its great grain elevators on the horizon.

Campillos, we decided as we rode in, was the ugliest, least interesting town we had ever seen in Spain. The grain elevators dominated it; in fact they were its sole reason for existence. It is the only town I have ever seen with only half a plaza, for the main dirt road which ran straight past the grain elevators and so on to the mountains at the far horizon simply widened on one side to make a little dusty square. There were a couple of cafés, the *posada* next to the railroad station, a garage with three or four tractors standing outside, a substantial quantity of houses, two churches and nothing else. On every side stretched endless fields of wheat—Iowa or Kansas.

Had our next day's stop not been so very far away I would have been tempted to ride on, but we might have found ourselves lost in the foothills by nightfall. So we made the best of it and wrote it off as one day that, except for the beautiful girl, we could regard as a total loss.

That night we sat outside the *posada* drinking beer and watching the farmers drive in and out of town on their little farm tractors, apparently the evening's only diversion in Campillos. So early to bed. Now the seventeenth of October, we saddled up at first light and shook off the dust of this dusty little town, heading through Bobadilla and over a mountain pass to the ancient city of Antequera where we were to spend the night.

The first part of this day's ride led to Bobadilla, which is nothing but a junction point where the railroad from Madrid to the south divides, one section going through Córdoba to Sevilla, Jerez, San Fernando—the station for Cádiz—and on to the sea, ending at Algeciras across the bay from Gibraltar. The other branch goes off to Granada and terminates in Málaga.

As this is a junction point and trains and travelers often have to wait to make connections, Bobadilla has a very large and beautiful station with a façade set with the finest of tiles in the true Moorish blue in very fanciful designs. Often, riding the *ferrocarril* from Madrid to Málaga, I have awakened at dawn in Bobadilla and, peering sleepily out of my berth, admired this impressive station, wondering what sort of charming city lay behind it. Now I found out. There is the station, a roundhouse, innumerable sidings, lines of freight cars waiting to go off in various directions, about forty houses, the glorious railroad station and nothing, nothing else at all.

We stopped at the station where I went in, thinking, for I had seen the lines, that I could surely send off a telegram to my wife in California simply to show her I had been there, but even that was impossible; the telegraph was only for railroad use.

We now cut across the valley and during the afternoon, gradually mounting through wooded and most pleasant country, passing through occasional small villages, finally came out at about five o'clock on the main Sevilla highway which we followed for a mile or so into the city of Antequera.

This was one of the key cities of Andalucía from the very earliest times but is now a modern and industrial center from which principal highways diverge in all directions, Córdoba, Granada, Sevilla, Málaga, so we didn't intend to do more than spend the night, and I had no intention of taking a pack train through its busy streets.

Just at the point where we rode into town there is a very good government *parador,* or inn, so Greg and I decided to spend the night there, enjoy another infrequent hot both, and let the boys take the horses on into town to the *posada.* I told them to get the horses out the other side of town in the morning to a spot where, about half a mile beyond the city limits, a country lane, a *camino vaquero,* diverged from the highway and would lead us up into the mountains on our road to Teba. We would take a taxi and meet them there.

The *posada* here was the same one that had sheltered Washington Irving and his companion a hundred and thirty-five years before, and here the great author most amusingly missed the point of a Spanish story. He was listening to the innkeeper, and I quote:

"There was once a fountain, he said, in one of the public squares, called 'La Fuente del Toro,' the fountain of the bull, because the water gushed from the mouth of a bull's head carved of stone. Underneath the head was inscribed:

*En frente del toro*
*Se halla tesoro.*

" 'In front of the bull there is treasure.' Many dug in front of the fountain, but lost their labor and found no money. At last one knowing fellow construed the motto a different way. It is in the forehead (*frente*) of the bull that the treasure is to be found, said he to himself, and I am the man to find it. Accordingly he came late at night, and knocked the head to pieces; and what do you think he found?

" 'Plenty of gold and diamonds!' cried Sancho eagerly.

" 'He found nothing,' rejoined mine host dryly; 'and he ruined the fountain.'

"Here a great laugh was set up by the landlord's hangers-on who considered Sancho completely taken in by what I presume was one of mine host's standing jokes."

77

Apparently our good author had no great knowledge of the bull-fight, was not an *aficionado,* for to us the Spanish *double-entendre* was obvious. The real meaning of the quotation is that treasure is to be found only face to face, *a frente,* with the bull; in other words, rewards are not for cowards.

The next day we were up at seven, had our coffee, and took the cab down to the junction. The horses had not yet arrived, so Greg and I went over and squatted against the wall of a big two-story house that stood right at the corner where our path left the paved highway.

There now occurred one of those pleasant experiences that, at least for me, highlighted the trip.

There was quite a chill wind blowing around the corner and along the front of the house from Greg to me. I was about ten yards, thank God, to leeward of him as we leaned against the wall trying to warm ourselves in the first rays of the morning sun. Suddenly I heard Greg let out a yell and a curse. Looking up, I saw, in a second-story window a little to windward of him, the startled face of a dear little old lady who had just emptied a chamber pot on his defenseless head! I don't know which was the more horrified, Greg or the old lady, I was too weak from laughing. For the rest of the trip and afterward this was always referred to as the *"Ante-quera Bon Voyage."*

Our two cowboys turned up now with the led horses and naturally joined in the laughter at Greg's expense. Burgo called it a *"mal-fortuna de mañana"* and cautioned poor Greg against walking too close to walls of houses in the morning in any Spanish country town.

The *camino vaquero* led us comfortably away from the highway and its dangerous traffic and through pleasant groves of cork trees up into the hills. These drovers' roads, when you hit them, make for very pleasant voyaging. They are not regularly defined roads but usually an area about twenty yards wide, grassy under foot,

78

bounded by rough stone walls to keep driven cattle out of the crops. All morning we enjoyed fine riding, stopping only once to reset a loose hind shoe on Greg's horse. We carried blacksmith's pincers and a rasp, so with a couple of rocks and a hammer this was soon done, and we were on our way, the road gradually petering out into a trail as we approached our first mountain pass.

Here our trail met the highway again in a narrow gorge. Gingerly following the road, slippery footing at best, we encountered a drover with three pack mules. He told us that he knew the country well and that there was absolutely no way across the pass other than by following the pavement. So we started two hours of nerve-racking travel along the edge of the road bedeviled by passing trucks and automobiles. I particularly hate this sort of riding. One is always under tension, the horses unsure of themselves, every corner, especially on a grade, a potential hazard. Nothing is more tiring.

Once over this pass, we came into a valley of olive groves and were able at last to ride carefree among the trees for a couple of hours, but then we hit the pass above Teba and the same thing occurred again. We followed the highway to where we could see the town across the valley sitting in a cup between two mountains. It seemed to be about five miles away.

Here we were stopped again by a pair of Guardia Civil to check our papers. I asked them if there was any way of getting up to Teba without following the damned paved roads. They said no, but if we were going on to Loja and Granada they could put us on a mountain trail that would take us eventually to Loja, passing through several villages without once having to meet the paved road again.

From a distance Teba looked most picturesque and inviting, but, after considering the harrowing day that we had passed, the trail looked more inviting than a further two hours on the highway, followed by at least as much more the following morning. So Greg took several long-distance scenic shots of the town and we headed thankfully off into the hills.

In a way I was disappointed at not visiting this town for besides being the titular home of the Conde Jimmy de Teba, Spain's greatest shot, the son of the late "Doña Sol," the fabulous sister of the late James, Duke of Alba, Teba is also one of the titles of Eugenia de Montijo, Empress of France, and probably is full of interesting mementos of this famous family.

The trail ran on down the mountain into a good dirt road passing scattered farms. Here in the late afternoon we had an amusing if slightly annoying diversion. A mule staked out in a field, seeing us come by, broke loose and joined us happily. As so often happens with mules, he fell slavishly in love with our pack mare and insisted on following obstinately and dumbly at her heels in spite of all our efforts to drive him away. When one of these damned animals forms such an attachment he will follow the object of his affections for miles. This is why a train of pack mules is usually led by a bell-mare. We did not want to turn up in Granada with an extra mule, and as we knew the poor owner would be looking for it there was nothing to do but stop while Benítez and Burgo each selected a hatful of rocks with which they stoned the wretched animal over the hills and out of sight. In half an hour he came bursting out of the brush again and took up his adoring position at the mare's heels.

Four times we had to stop and chase that wretched nuisance all over the countryside, throwing stones at him. Four times he slavishly returned, consumed by frustrated love. Finally after losing hell's own time we came to a man plowing a field. This good fellow not only knew the mule but he had an extra picket rope, so he tied our tormented lover to a tree and said he would return it to its owner when he went home that evening.

81

By this time we had lost so many hours to bad roads and our four-legged friend that to make Loja was absolutely out of the question. Dusk was coming on us; we were tired, cold and disgruntled. Ahead of us was a tiny village with a cement quarry and a few houses. We decided to spend the night there even if we had to camp out.

The place was called Salinas and it was on a dirt road of sorts that served the quarry. We rode in and explained our situation to the foreman. There was no real stabling, but as we wanted to get the horses in out of the cold he very kindly drove his two trucks out of the garage and arranged to bed the horses there for the night. While this was going on, with the usual courteousness he put out two chairs from his house for us, and his wife brought us out glasses of coffee and some cheese and sliced sausage. The kindness of these people is endless.

The cowboys were going to sleep in our bedding rolls with the horses, while for us two beds were found over the tiny bar that served the village.

All the inhabitants of Salinas are powdered, skin, hair and clothing, completely white from the cement in which they work, and that night as we ate the simple dinner that the bartender's wife cooked for us it was like sitting in a room full of albinos. These people see very few passers-by, and quite a few citizens crowded into the little bar that night to hear about our journey. Finally, quite late, one old man insisted that the bartender's wife bring out the daughter of the house to dance for us. Imagine our surprise when the entertainer, clad in diapers and a nightshirt, proved to be just two years old!

The patrons began singing and clapping their hands to an *alegria,* and to our amazement this tiny tot began dancing not only beautifully but with such simpers and seductive flashing glances that we realized the instinct of charming starts very early among Spanish women.

The scene in the shadowy cantina, the rustic singers showing a serious appreciation of the artistry of the dancing child, reminded me of a report penned by the English traveler Swinburne. This contemporary of Beckford said in his *Travels in Spain, 1775–1776*: "Every Spaniard may be said to be born with it in head and heels; I have seen a child of three years of age dance it to the mother's singing, with steps and turns scarce to be credited in an infant of that age." This little Spaniard was willing apparently to keep it up as long as the applause lasted, but we, tiring before she did, stumbled off to bed.

The following morning, the nineteenth, I found that the dirt road would only put us back onto the highway beyond Teba, so I tried to find someone to guide us over the passes to Loja by the mountain trail. One man who had a mule offered to lead us over for two hundred pesetas, but Burgo declared that this price was exorbitant, so we refused and decided to trust to luck and get our information from ranch to ranch or by chance encounter along the way. It worked out very well.

We rode steadily up through the mountains from village to farm with no trouble all day long. As we approached the *Vega* of Granada the country became more beautiful and varied, the greater abundance was noticeable, and the hard flinty bones of Spain covered with a deeper and richer soil. No wonder the Moors clung to this rich region until the bloody bitter end under the walls of the Alhambra.

It was interesting to us that as we asked our way and explained our journey almost all but the most ignorant of people seemed to know about Washington Irving. This was true during the whole trip. Some had no idea who he was, but that a man of that name had ridden through an undetermined number of years before was either hearsay or legend. Curiously some people imagined that their fathers had seen him. As hardly anyone we spoke to—I really think no one—had ever read a translation of his famous book, the man obviously has become part of Andalucian folklore. The nearer we came to Granada the more contemporary the great writer became. By the time we reached Santa Fé we almost expected to see the dust of his passage in the air before us.

Eight hours down the mountains with one short stop brought us into the wonderful city of Loja, wedged into its crevice in the last pass before Granada. I had often admired it from the automobile road far above but had never been down into this picturesque place.

As we rode into this rich, substantial city, fine houses, churches and public buildings on every side indicated the importance it has had for so many centuries. From the fine sweeping central plaza the street narrowed and became stepped, so we dismounted and led down to where, facing the market place, a most imposing *posada* welcomed us.

This building, three stories high, must have at one time been a palace, for two great fluted Romanesque columns framed its central archway over which was a large armorial shield, a façade of imposing if decayed elegance. The market square on which it faced was Roman with some of the columns still standing integrated into the house fronts. Neatly clipped plane trees outlined this plaza across which was a comfortable old-fashioned hotel where Greg and I elected to spend the night.

After we had unpacked our saddlebags Greg took his camera and went off to get some pictures around the market while I went back to find the telegraph office and also to check into a bookshop that I had noticed as we came in, for a good bookseller is usually a valuable source of information. I wasn't disappointed, for this is some of what I found out.

Situated in a gorge opening onto the *Vega* of Granada, Loja had always been a fortress, a key to the city, and as such has had a long and most turbulent history of raids and sieges, burnings, destruction and rebuilding going back to prehistoric days.

Under the Romans this city was called Illipula Laus. During

those times the then bishop, Estéfano, and three hundred Christians were martyred by Roman compatriots in 47 A.D. The Arabs, conquering it in 721, burned it and put the populace to the sword. They also changed its name to Isnalojaque, from which the modern name of Loja derives. In 889 it fell again in an Arab civil war to King Zaide of Granada who took it away from the Caliphate of Córdoba to which it had owed allegiance. Once again the flames of its destruction were reflected in the blood running in its gutters. A stormy history.

Granada ruled it until 1224, when King Ferdinand III of Sevilla stormed and again destroyed it. In the same year the Moors retook it with great carnage and rebuilt the city on the old ruins. In 1361, a little over a hundred years later, Loja changed hands again. In 1431 the Moors recaptured it for the last time and held it until 1486, fifty-five years later, when the unhappy town, after a great battle on the fields of Lucena by the river below the city, fell to the arms of Ferdinand and Isabella.

So this now lovely town has run with blood, leaped with flames, heard the screams of the butchered for centuries. No wonder the Moors called it "The Cockpit of Granada"! Who would guess it now?

After such a history of destruction there is of course very little of the Moorish influence remaining in Loja. The town as we see it today is a modern Spanish city, if one considers the early sixteenth century as modern, for it is from the earliest decades of that century that Loja was last rebuilt.

The dominating feature of the town is the Alcazaba. This is a great rock towering in the center of the city the crown of which has always been fortified, but the Roman and Arab forts have been built on and superseded by the present Spanish fortress of that time. Its first Spanish *alcaide,* or commander, was Don Alvaro de Luna. This office descended by inheritance and marriages through the families of de Rozal, Pérez de Meca, and from them to the noble house of the Condes de San Julián who hold it at present. The principal church in Loja is the Iglesia de Santa María de la Encarnación. This great Gothic edifice was commenced in 1501 on the foundations of the old Moorish mosque, which at the reconquest was ordered destroyed by King Ferdinand.

A young Spanish friend whose rational and deductive thinking I greatly respect once remarked, "When I recall how great a Moorish civilization we destroyed in this Peninsula, I can only wish, Jimmy, that the reconquest had taken place three hundred years later. Had Napoleon expelled the Moors rather than Ferdinand and Isabella, Spanish culture would have been immeasurably enriched." This church was completed in seven years, a remarkably short time for a work of such magnitude. It has an interior of great splendor; the magnificent choir is designed by Coro, and among the statues and images it contains are some of the finest works of Alonso Cano.

As Loja is a good-sized town of over 25,000 people, it naturally has many places of interest, among them the church of San Gabriel and the ancient monastery of Santa Clara, which was also built in 1515. But as I am not trying to write a guide book of the city, and certainly could not in two short days, I can only say it is well worth a visit for anyone who finds himself in the vicinity of Granada.

As we were saddling up for the last stage of our trip we were lucky to find that another patron of the *posada*, a well-to-do farmer, was about to set out for his *finca* which was situated on our route. He had two of the finest mules one could imagine, riding one and leading the other packed with supplies that he had been purchasing. This pleasant man showed us the way out of town across the river to the well-traveled *camino vaquero* that would lead us toward Granada. Now that we were in the *vega,* all highly cultivated, our problem was to find our way, which involved many changes of

direction, in order to reach our goal with the minimum of highway travel.

This day was perfectly delightful riding, but I must say without our friend's lead we could have been either hopelessly lost or caught in the heavy traffic of main roads long before he left us at the village of Puente de los Vaqueros.

By now there was water everywhere. Everything was under intense cultivation; groves of fruit trees and almonds, fields of maize, truck gardens and small villages abounded. One unforgettable sight was a very large series of threshing floors where the farmers were sorting out different-colored maize, making large patterns like a quilt of red, orange, gold and black cobs of maize. Greg got some beautiful colored pictures of this lovely sight.

Two or three miles beyond this place our track separated into four or five footpaths. There was no one around of whom to ask directions, but all were vaguely pointing toward Granada, so we took one at random and in half an hour found ourselves completely lost in a birch forest. This wasn't a natural forest but an enormous planted grove, and the path we had chosen was obviously only a woodcutter's way of getting to the trees, for some of them had been harvested in strips and were stacked beside the path which ended there. There was no point in retracing our way, so we kept on riding through the pleasant shade always in the general direction of our goal, hoping to stumble on a more reasonable road. Eventually we came to a little river, and I knew it had to lead into the middle of the *vega* somewhere as there is only one main river running from Granada to the sea; we followed downstream along its banks.

After a mile or two we came to a ford which was well traveled and showed fresh damp wheel tracks. We crossed it and, sure enough, in a short time we overtook two bullock carts creaking slowly along. They made a most charming picture. In front was a young countryman leading the patient slow-pacing oxen with his goad resting across their tasseled yokes, the high tilted canvas covers of the cart like sails of ships on some deep shadowed sea, the lazy puffs of dust hanging in the windless air of the early afternoon. In the second cart, driven by the young wife, two little boys, eyes gleaming diamond-bright, were peering out; between the wheels, elegant as Diana, a greyhound bitch, mauve in the shadows, paced gracefully along. Nets slung under the axles held fodder for the night's stop. As we drew alongside this gentle procession the usual courtesies went back and forth:

*"Vayan con Dios, caballeros."*

*"Con Dios, señor."*

This little caravan turned out to be the whole property of the young farmer who was moving his family to a new farm which his father had just bought.

Greg remarked that with a few garlands on the carts and wreathes of flowers around the bullocks' necks they could have been on their way to join a *Romería*. Of course they lacked the pretty girls in dancing dresses, the strumming guitars, and we in our travel-worn clothes were no example of the chic horsemen who canter and circle around such a procession, for a *Romería* is most elegant indeed.

To explain Greg's jest, I must tell you what a *Romería* is.

This type of festival is typical to Andalucía. In the rural districts of southern Spain when spring is well advanced and planting ended a natural restiveness stirs in the blood. The air is fresh, the nights are balmy, and the thoughts of the sensual Andalúz turn most intelligently to pleasure and religion.

By some happy chance at this season of the year various shrines and holy places see fit to celebrate fiesta. From far and near the countrymen come to assist at the celebration. On every farm the largest two-wheeled hay-cart is brought out, whitewashed and gaily painted. A fresh white cotton cover is draped over its hoops and decorated with flowers and garlands. The oxen, beautifully groomed and also flower-wreathed, are inspanned; the cart, filled with quilts, cooking utensils and food and finally packed with girls and women all in lovely flounced dancing dresses, is ready to set out. The men in their best *traje corto,* eyes shaded by the wide *sombrero ancho,* mount their finest horses; somebody strikes up on a guitar, and to songs and music the family moves off to join with others in a long and happy procession, sometimes on a voyage of as much as four days. A glorious picnic to the shrine of their choice.

Each night's encampment is a fiesta in itself. Very little time is given to sleeping. All night long there is dancing around the campfires as the wineskins pass from hand to hand. Inpromptu horse racing and wrestling bouts naturally lead to friendly fights, for every man has to prove he is more "*macho*", more virile, than the next. Sometimes as many as fifty carts, which means several hundred people, may be in one *Romería,* so you can imagine how gay and colorful these traveling villages can be.

Obviously a festival as jolly as this is far too much fun to be left only to the farmers, so, long since, the rest of us have all joined in. When I say all, I mean all who are young enough and stubborn enough not to mind a few sleepless days and nights!

Some of these *Romerías* have become very important over the years, achieving a far more than local reputation. Not far from Granada in the Sierra Morena, home of wolves and wild boars, there is a famous shrine to the Virgen de la Cabeza which is the scene of a most spectacular yearly procession. This *Romería* attracts people from as far as a hundred miles away. The towns and villages through which the carts and riders wind their way all decorate for the occasion and play host to the passing pilgrims. Each night is a village fair and each morning sees last night's hosts, weary but happy, harness up and join their guests, swelling

the caravan as it wanders through the hills to the following evening's gaiety.

By the time the constantly growing procession arrives at the sanctuary hundreds of people are prepared to camp around its walls to join in the holy rites that follow. The image of the Virgin is known affectionately as "La Morenita," which means the "Young Girl of the Sierra Morena." Beautifully robed and decked in all her jewels, she is carried in procession all about the shrine; around her wave the holy banners of the *confradias,* the religious fraternities; the women walking and the horsemen all carry yard-long tapers lighted at the shrine. So night and day, with beating drums and the wild cry of the bugles, with singing and dancing, the Holy Mother is celebrated for that year.

Another great procession even more famous is the Romería del Rocío which has its origin in Sevilla. Its route roughly follows the course of the River Guadalquivir and ends on an island in the marshes not far from Huelva. This lasts for three days, is very gay, and most of the girls pack four or five dancing dresses; these dresses are usually covered with big polka dots, gypsy fashion, with rows and rows of heavy flounces.

An amiable bull-breeding friend, Tomás Prieto de la Cal, Marqués de Seona, has his *ganadería* between Huelva and El Rocío, where he not only raises some of the largest fighting bulls in Spain but happily extends the widest welcome. For some years past, thanks to this goodhearted friend, it is possible to pamper one's aging bones by sleeping at Tomás' in comfortable beds and riding over to El Rocío for the daily festivities, leaving the young to do the camping out. Tomás raises bulls of such size and ferocity that he has a hard time selling them, but luckily he is wealthy enough to indulge his passion of breeding bulls to the old classic standard. The result of this is that his *novillos* or three-year-olds are nearly the size of a full-grown bull. Some time past I saw a *novillada* of

93

these animals fought in Madrid. It was fantastic. The first bull sent his *novillero* to the infirmary; the second boy killed that one and was in turn hospitalized by his bull. The third *torero* killed the second bull, then took on his own, was in turn gored, and the afternoon ended with three men in the infirmary and four bulls unkilled! *"Qué barbaridad!"*

So much for *romerías*. Reminiscences of pilgrimages and *corridas* long since fought have led us a long way from our little cavalcade winding through the shady valley. The young farmer told us that not far ahead lay the village of Puente de los Vaqueros, Bridge of the Cowboys, where he planned to spend the night, for he had been on the way since dawn and the oxen needed resting. If we could suit our pace to his he would be happy to show us to our next turnoff, an inconspicuous path and very easy to overlook. This seemed a sensible idea, besides which we were enjoying the company of this picturesque little family, especially Greg, who was getting lots of charming photographs of the children, carts and oxen as we rode along. Whenever he spotted a particularly attractive setup ahead, he would canter forward and line up his proposed picture and get good shots as we came riding by.

The young Andalúz, whose name turned out to be Abelardo Suárez, proved a most entertaining fellow. About twenty-eight years old, he had been born and raised on his father's farm in a mountain valley about fifteen miles away; there he had married, started his little family, and spent the years working for the old man who, from what he said, must have been quite prosperous.

"Beyond Puente de los Vaqueros, señor, on the banks of the Río Genil is the little village of Chauchina. Here my late aunt, God rest her, had a very good farm. This good woman, Tia Pépé, a widow, dying childless, left this farm to her brothers, my father and my uncle. This uncle, a townsman, occupies himself with a small cantina on the outskirts of Illora; he has no interest in agriculture,

so my father, who had a little *dinero* put by, bought him out and by my great good fortune has given this farm to be mine. So we go now, the *mujer,* the little ones and I, to make our new life.

"Who knows? Perhaps by the Grace of God I shall prosper sufficiently, enlarge myself enough so that, in God's good time, I may leave to each of my sons a farm when I am gone."

Who knows? I only pray this good man's wish comes true. When I think of that happy little family with such a quiet and pleasant future ahead of them in one of the most delightful situations in the world, it really makes me wonder if they aren't looking forward to an ideal life.

*"Buena suerte, Don Abelardo. Good luck, man!"*

By the time we got to Puente de los Vaqueros we were riding along a fine dirt road shaded by handsome poplar trees. Our instinct would have been to ride straight on this pleasant way, but luckily before he left us our guide pointed out a tiny path between two houses and told us to keep on it and not to go to the right or left and we would find ourselves on another serviceable road. We soon were riding through back yards, kitchen gardens, the footpath finally dwindling to a narrow dyke which led me to think we must have lost our way. Eventually this became a path running through a long grove of young birch trees. After a couple of miles I was sure that we must be completely lost, but we crossed a broad shallow stream and there was a beautiful grass-carpeted, shaded road, like a ride through a forest in France, heading straight along in the proper direction. We silently thanked our friend and enjoyed a couple of hours of cool easy going.

All morning we could see in a fold of the foothills on our left hand the beautiful white city of Illora shining like a jumble of sugar cubes against this rosy background. I had wanted to pass through it, but closer familiarity with local conditions changed my mind; all the information I could get proved that we would only

96

find ourselves enmeshed in a web of paved highways again if we tried to reach it. This made us miss an anticipated visit to the vast estate of the Wellington family who, as Marqueses de Douro, hold it as a grant from the Spanish Crown as a reward to their illustrious ancestor for his victories in the peninsular wars. Major Thomsen, who manages the estate, had been most helpful in assisting me to lay out the last portion of my ride and I was very keen to see him again, but by this time paved highways had become such an anathema that I felt it wiser to press on. The Wellingtons also hold an enormous grant between Guadiaro and San Roque on the southern coast—I believe one of the largest cork forests in the world.

In this way, directed from village to village, we gradually moved nearer to our goal. We had a little trouble because each time we would ask our way the first reaction of the inhabitants would be to direct us by the shortest route to the Santa Fé-Granada highway, which was just what we did not want, but with great good luck we managed to keep on these back tracks until quite late in the afternoon we hit the paved road again about three miles from Santa Fé.

At this point, although we went up and down the road for a couple of hundred yards in each direction, we couldn't find any continuation of the bypath. While we were doing this a young man came along who was giving himself a rather thrilling afternoon teaching his girl friend how to ride a Vespa. He looked quite ter-rified behind her. We hailed him, congratulated him on his cour-age, and asked if he knew any way of bypassing Santa Fé. He didn't. It was now getting to be five o'clock in the afternoon and I didn't look forward to doing the last fifteen miles to Granada on a heavily traveled highway at night.

From here on I knew what faced us very well for I had made many a trip by car from Santa Fé into Granada, so I suggested to

Greg that we leave the horses at Santa Fé and take a taxi into the Alhambra Palace Hotel for the night.

In Granada I have a good old friend, a taxi driver named Pedro Padilla. For many years he has driven us each spring when we come to that beautiful city for three days of *corridas* during the Feast of Corpus Cristi. Padilla is a born Granadino; he knows more about the city and its environs than anyone else I know. My idea was to get Pedro early the next morning, find out where the Granada *posada* was, and from there have him show us exactly the dirt roads that would run to Santa Fé. Then we could go on, pick up the horses about ten o'clock, and have a pleasant and safe ride all the way in.

The plan worked beautifully. Pedro came to the hotel after dinner, delighted to see me, and when I explained what I wanted he said he would pick us up the following morning and show us the exact route, as he had lived all over the valley as a boy and could put us on a road that would take us directly into town without a single piece of pavement. This was a godsend and we slept easier that night.

The following morning off we went with Pedro, first to the *posada* where we had made reservations. From there he drove us two blocks and showed us several large stretches of open land we could cross where they were going to build apartment houses. Beyond this terrain was the main highway from Granada to Motril, but this had a wide unpaved walkway all the way, shaded by trees, a sort of sidewalk which would carry us safely out of the traffic. We drove down the Motril highway and turned in behind a big jam factory. The plant abutted on a dry river bed, very wide and sandy. We memorized the location. Now we retraced our steps up to the Santa Fé highway. Pedro drove down it for about three miles and showed us a nice dirt road bisecting the highway we were on.

This road, he said, would lead us into the river bed about two hundred yards below the jam factory. So far so good. We then went back to the Santa Fé highway and continued on our way. After another three or four miles he again turned off and drove us down to a little village. Here he showed us where the jam-factory road made a dog-legged turn across the highway and went on toward Santa Fé. We repeated this maneuver twice more; each time our dirt road had to cross the highway, if we had to make a jog we noted it. Finally we arrived at Santa Fé and the invaluable Pedro showed us exactly where the unpaved road began.

We found Burgo and Benítez with the horses all saddled and ready and, thanks to our foresight, enjoyed a pleasant, carefree finale to our ride.

The *vega* of Granada is one of the richest in Spain and that morning our route was through beautiful fruit groves and flower gardens with rippling brooks on either side, for the eternal snow of the Sierra Nevada gives boundless water to this valley all year round. Ahead of us, all gray and rose, was the beautiful city crowned by the fantastic bulk of the greatest Moorish monument in Europe, the Alhambra.

Farm succeeded prosperous farm. Some of the way led through fields of tobacco, some through rich market gardens. Pedro Padilla's careful instructions kept us safely on the correct road; without them we would have been hopelessly lost in all this abundance. Finally we came to the dry river bed and followed up it to our welcoming jam factory. I must say they were a bit surprised to see our small travel-worn cavalcade wind through their camion park. So up the Motril road and into town.

To end with the proper flourish I suppose we should have ridden straight through this handsome city and up into the forecourt of the Alhambra. But the very heavy traffic, both tourist and local, punctuated by numerous traffic signals, and the paved conditions of the roads up the hill and through the beautiful park to the palace gateway made this impractical if not impossible.

Instead we rode directly to the *posada,* our final *posada,* dis-

99

mounted and unsaddled for the last time. For the first time in a hundred and thirty-five years a group of riders had come that whole long distance. For us "The Journey" was ended; I couldn't help feeling a bit sad. It was good to have made the ride, but I would have loved to be starting all over again.

It wasn't easy to say good-by to the good horses who had carried us faithfully over the hundreds of kilometers of good going and bad, and we certainly both regretted to see the last of Benítez and Burgo. The latter especially, who had borne all the responsibility of the trip on his broad and willing shoulders. Day by day his skill had kept us going safely, his cheerfulness and good nature had eased our road. A great horseman, his temperament made him also a faithful servant and most pleasant *compañero*.

Don José Burgo Ramírez, wherever you are, *"Vaya con Dios, caballero!"*

When visiting Granada I always try to stay at the old Alhambra Palace Hotel in rooms on the town side, for from their balconies you can look down over the whole city spread almost like a map before you. Down the hill to your left you see the palaces and gardens of the wealthy, locally known as *"carménes."* A good many of these were palaces of the Moorish nobles with rose gardens, fountains and reflecting pools shaded by enormous ancient cypresses which are so typical of this the most beautiful city in Spain. They delight the eye, a rose and green pattern majestically stepping down to the great tree-lined avenue along the riverbank where the fairs are held.

Directly in front of you a most picturesque little street zigzags down the hill. This is the street of the lacemakers; outside of every house you can see them busily at work, for from here come the most beautiful mantillas in the country. Tastefully hanging along the walls are the finest examples of their art, some rose, some yellow, but mostly black or white. One luscious temptation leads you to the next, and we who live in Spain make it a rule, if possible, never to let our wives walk down this street—it's ruinous! This little *callé* ends in a most amusing square. Nicely shaded by gigantic plane trees, surrounded on three sides by substantial-looking old houses, now mostly apartments, its fourth boundary is the Emergency Hospital. I have spent hours with my field glasses just watching the life and activity with which this plaza abounds.

It is a microcosm of the city; in front of its one café there is constant coming and going, greetings, salutations and arguments. Two or three vendors' stalls can always attract their share of bargaining women. Underfoot and among the trees bands of children, mostly dressed in spotless white, romp happily. To one side a group of boys will be skillfully kicking a football. All at once far off in the town you hear the distant wail of a siren. Instantly the plaza reacts!

From the café the loungers begin to wander across to the hospital entrance; the market women and their customers leave the stalls; the football game also moves slowly toward the hospital. As the sound of the siren grows louder and nearer the surrounding houses disgorge their quota of the inquisitive. By the time the ambulance draws up at the entrance, two lines of appreciative connoisseurs of misfortune stretch from the portal to where the unfortunate victim is being unloaded. As the stretcher is carried between the lines of curious faces everyone takes a knowing look at the patient. This little drama is played out several times a day, so you can see that these onlookers are not ghouls, just experts, each considering him or herself an infallible diagnostician of all human fallibility.

The great portals clang shut and the crowd disperses into happy little groups comparing notes. Did you see it? That my eyes should behold . . . but the legs, María, did you see the legs? Let the Lord have mercy . . . Was it grave? *Gravísimo, hombre, una barbaridad!* Everyone goes about his business in the comforting knowledge of a delightful conversational topic for the next couple of hours when, with luck, the siren will be heard again.

For anyone who enjoys, as I do, while unobserved, a peak at life, I recommend a strong pair of field glasses. You may be sure I am not the first such Peeping Tom to practice in Granada. I quote from Washington Irving:

"I have spoken of a balcony of the central window of the Hall of Ambassadors. It served as a kind of observatory where I used often to take my seat, and consider not merely the heaven above but the earth beneath. Besides the magnificent prospect which it commanded of mountain, valley and vega, there was a little busy scene of human life laid open to inspection immediately below. At the foot of the hill was an alameda or public walk which, though not so fashionable as the more modern and splendid paseo of the Xenil, still boasted a varied and picturesque concourse. Hither resorted the small gentry of the suburbs together with priests and friars, who walked for appetite and digestion; machos and majas, the beaux and belles of the lower classes in their Andalusian dress; swaggering contrabandistas, and sometimes half muffled and mysterious loungers of the higher ranks, on some secret assignation.

"It was a moving picture of Spanish life and character, which I delighted to study; and as the astronomer has his grand telescope with which to sweep the skies, and, as it were, bring the stars nearer for his inspection, so I had a smaller one, of pocket size, for the use of my observatory, with which I could sweep the regions below, and bring the countenances of the motley groups so close as almost, at times, to make me think I could define their conversation by the play and expression of their features. I was thus, in a manner, an invisible observer, and without quitting my solitude, could throw myself in an instant into the midst of society, a rare advantage to one of somewhat shy and quiet habits, and fond, like myself, of observing the drama of life without becoming an actor in the scene."

As my balcony was approximately halfway down the hill of the Alhambra from Washington Irving's "observatory," I delight to think that it was my very plaza that gave to the great author such clandestine pleasure.

Beyond this lively plaza you see the heart of the city of Granada dominated by the great gray bulk of the cathedral, which leads the eye through the modern business district of the city, on past the *plaza de toros*, the verdant suburbs, to the *Vega* where, far in the distance, shimmer the spires of Santa Fé.

To the right across the valley rears the opposite hill of the Albaicín. The whole of this little mountain is still covered with the Moorish city completely intact, most blessedly unchanged. Most of the streets are far too narrow to negotiate by car and many of them are stepped besides; however, I have made one trip to Pedro Padilla's little taxi from the plaza at the top all the way down to the foot. It was at night and the narrow lanes were nearly empty, but still it was an experience comparable to running the *Cresta* and I wouldn't recommend anyone trying it! Still further along the hill just out of sight of the hotel are the famous gypsy caves about which one hears so much. Here the *gitanos* live. In these picturesque surroundings, comfortable in their well-publicized homes, beautifully costumed in all of their flamenco finery, they entertain the eager tourists with some of the worst, the phoniest singing and dancing to be heard east of Chicago.

I have described earlier in this book the tremendous importance of inspiration, of "*duende*", in true flamenco art; here in the caves of Albaicín the inspiration is furnished entirely by money and a bottle of *manzanilla*. At the sound of the tourists' cars coming to a halt below, bright smiles light each expectant face and, like well-trained entertainers, they go into their act. In twenty minutes by the clock inspiration leaves them, they collect their money, and so back to their knitting until the next inspiring autos come along. It is worth it, nevertheless, at least for a first-time visitor, because the caves themselves are such amusing curiosities. This area of the caves was once the quarters of a group of Moorish refugees from Baeza. Here they congregated after the fall of Granada, and here they were massacred and the houses burned. Over the years the gypsies have moved into the ruins, so you can see they have been in possession for about four hundred years, and in four hundred years an imaginative gypsy can make quite a thing out of what started as a simple hole in a cliff.

Neat and well-tended paths wind back and forth up the face of the hill, and along these midget avenues open the caves, like houses along a street. Nothing will grow in this rocky soil, but tasteful, colorful potted gardens grace each façade. These are not caves in the wild sense but commodious troglodyte dwellings, with conventional doorways and windows cut into the cliff face. Both outside and inside are always freshly whitewashed, and usually a brightly colored hand-woven Andalúz counterpane, fringed and tasseled, curtains the doorway. Entering, the visitor finds himself in a good-sized *sala* or living room furnished with sufficient rush-bottomed chairs to seat the entertainers and their little audience. On the walls hang lurid religious chromos, bullfight posters and beautiful examples of the copperware for which these tribes are famous. Interestingly enough, they will never sell any of this copper from their houses, but it is all for sale at open-air stalls or little shops around about the city. From this main room bedrooms and a kitchen branch out, and you can often see, sleeping through the noisy entertainment, two or three children huddled together in one bed. Of course all these caves are electrically lighted, and I even heard, though never proved, that one of them has a bathroom! I must say it is a far cry from all this to sitting in some dingy back-street cantina and watching a great guitarist transform a skinny barefoot girl into a tempestuous, frenzied, great artist before your eyes. In all fairness, however, I must admit that these colorful performers in the caves of Granada answer a purpose. It would be utterly impossible for the casual tourist to take the time, to find the opportunity, to hit the lucky moment of an inspired *noche flamenco*. Perhaps I have been spoiled; after all, these singers and dancers do give the traveler a good example of the gypsy art during the short time that he can spare.

That afternoon I had to arrange for trucking the horses and men back to Jerez while Greg needed to replace some of his used film, so we decided that after a siesta we would go downtown and leave the Alhambra for following days. At this point, just having mentioned the siesta, may I diverge a moment to give the reader some advice. This is a bit of information, seemingly unimportant, which has proved invaluable to many of my friends; remember that during the hours of rest, the siesta, all Spain shuts tight. From one till four or half past in the afternoon not one civic office, no church, not a single museum, in fact nothing that could interest the traveler is open. Another point—there are almost no motorists and never any camions on the roads. For this reason I advise any hasty traveler, especially if limited for time, to spend these otherwise wasted hours in travel. You'll have them entirely to yourself.

Granada is a city so beautiful, so interesting, that no matter how often it is revisited its enchantment never palls. My companion and I decided to spend the following day enjoying the famous churches, shaded courts and lovely monuments that we knew so well. Although a visit to the fabled city was for us at least a yearly experience, its charm is always fresh. Like all wise travelers, we resisted the temptation of the Alhambra, no matter how strongly our desire drew us up the hill, for after that enchanted fortress, that unbelievable accumulation of aesthetic delight, every-

thing else is anticlimatic. I strongly advise any of my readers to remember this. Once you have wandered up the shady avenue through those dark majestic groves until the great red walls tower into the sky above you, once you have passed through the barbican into its courts you are bewitched and never again in the world can you admire other sights without invidious comparison. So leave it until the last.

Our first stop was at the great cathedral. This magnificent edifice is the work of the great architect Enrique de Égas who also built the Hospital Reál at Compostela, the holiest shrine in Spain. Here in Granada, in the Capilla Reál, lie the conquerors, Ferdinand and Isabella, their daughter Juana la Loca and her husband, Philip the Fair, the first Flemish king. The coffins are of course in a vault below, but the tombs with the effigies of the rulers were done in white marble by the Florentine sculptor Domenico Fancelli. An American can't help reflect on musing at the quiet marble figures that here lie the mother and the father of the New World.

In 1951 my wife and I were surprised to find in the Sacristy of this royal chapel a fresh exhibition of amazing Flemish paintings, among them an "Adoration of the Magi" by the Master of Bruges, a Memling Virgin, a Van der Weyden and many others of the same school. These pictures were in absolutely pristine condition; they looked to be fresh from the painter's brush. It was unbelievable! ! A thorough search on my wife's part proved that none of these paintings were catalogued. It was impossible to doubt their authenticity, especially the Memling, on which she is quite an authority. Later inquiries cleared up the mystery.

In 1950 the Pope had decreed a Holy Year and, expecting an influx of pilgrims, the cathedral, like many other European churches, had undertaken a thorough refurbishing. While working over the altar screen the artisans had uncovered these priceless paintings, still carefully packaged, stowed behind it. For four hundred and fifty years they had been hidden, unexposed to light, dust or candle smoke, hence their beautiful condition. It turned out that they had been the personal property of Isabella and had for centuries been considered lost by her in her years of campaigning against the Moors. The entire Sacristy has now been reorganized around this wonderful collection. A visit to it is an aesthetic experience not to be missed.

Another great building well worth visiting is the Cartuja or Charterhouse, the work of the architect Diego de Siloe, built in 1516. The very fine Baroque Sacristy contains the kneeling figure of the Gran Capitan, Gonzalo de Córdoba, conqueror of Naples, and of his wife, for they are buried here. The nave has some good paintings by Bocanegra and sculptures by Mora. One building which is also worth seeing is the Casa del los Tiros which has been made into a most exquisitely organized museum of provincial history. Here is gathered a wealth of Granadine examples and information, and I think that an hour or two profitably spent here is very helpful in laying a groundwork for any further exploration. In a short time you can pack in a solid foundation of knowledge of every facet of local life both present and historical, and it will add greatly to the enjoyment of your stay.

Two of the great festivals of Granada are the processions of Holy Week and the very splendid procession of the Blessed Sacrament on the day of Corpus Cristi, the last followed by three days of very fine bullfights.

If you are there for the fights of Corpus Cristi and are really interested in the *corrida,* it is worth while in the morning to go to an *apartado* or separation of the bulls. This ceremony takes place in the corrals adjacent to the bull ring at eleven o'clock in the morning before each fight and is forbidden to women as they are apt to make the bulls nervous. If you have no Spanish friends it is advisable to go with a good guide or taxi driver. For a small sum paid to the gatekeeper you can gain entrance to the *patio de caballos*, where you will find a large group of functionaries of the *Plaza de Toros, aficionados*, reporters and the confidential *banderilleros* of each matador. The last three are here to supervise the apportioning of the bulls for the afternoon's fights. This is always done most painstakingly and very fairly.

The six bulls for that day are in a small corral with walls about twenty feet high with a walkway and, thank God, a stout iron railing running along the top. Everyone now troops in up the outside stairs and takes their place along the walls, inspecting the bulls and discussing their various points, good or bad, in whispers so as not to disturb the nervous beasts. This is the great opportunity for *aficionados*, amateurs of bulls, and all manner of local wise guys to air their knowledge. While the quiet discussion may become general, the real work is being done by the three *banderilleros*, the *mayoral* or foreman of the bull ranch, the *mayoral* of the plaza and its *Presidente*. They are by common agreement dividing the six bulls into three equal lots. A very big difficult one may be paired with the smallest; a pair of extremely wide horns may be matched with, *toreros'* delight, a pair that point inward, and so forth, the idea being that any pair of bulls is as acceptable as any other pair. These men are all past masters at judging bulls and the discussion may last half an hour or more before it is settled to everyone's satisfaction. Then each pair of bulls is mentally given a number, one, two and three; these are written on cigarette papers which are rolled up and dropped into the foreman's sombrero and covered by another hat. The "confidential" of the senior matador of the afternoon reaches in and draws out the first number; the other two follow in order of seniority, then they all open their papers and see what the luck of the draw has brought them.

At this point the confidential *banderillero* begins to earn his pay. Those wise old eyes take in every trait of the two animals that have fallen to his lot. His employer, the matador, will never see these bulls until they burst out of the *toril* into the ring, and every bit of information he can get beforehand will be of immense value. It is up to this man, the most experienced in the *cuadrilla*, to decide which bull his *torero* will take first. Now another problem. The *toreros* fight in the order of their seniority which dates from the day they took their *alternativa* or presentation in the bull ring at Madrid. The senior will take the first and the fourth bull; the second will take numbers two and five, and the youngest in point of seniority will take three and six. The first man will be inclined to take his best bull last so that he can correct a bad impression. Knowing this, the second man may choose to fight his best bull first to make the first triumph of the afternoon, or he may not. The youngest has no choice; he must take his best bull first because the crowd may be leaving or at least not paying full attention by the time his second, the last bull of the afternoon, comes out. When you remember that nothing but the experience of the confidential *banderilleros* determines all these factors, you can see where an old man who has gotten a bit slow on his feet may still be the most important member of the team.

Once these decisions have been arrived at the most interesting phase of the *apartado* from the spectator's viewpoint commences, for the bulls have now to be moved from the corral into the fighting stalls in the exact order of their presentation. Remember that six creatures, all tiger wild, have to be moved with the utmost quiet and gentleness one by one through a series of complicated passages underneath the stands, until they are all in perfect sequence resting in the dark stalls, where they will remain totally undisturbed until they burst out into the sunlight of late afternoon.

This is done with a most complex series of trap doors which are swung to and fro by long ropes from the top of the corral walls. It requires the greatest patience for the bulls must be shifted around by voice call and softly tossed pebbles until the desired bull is nearest the gate. That gate is gently opened and the bull, sometimes by voice or if necessary by the glimpse of a man who steps out into the corral, exposing himself, is tempted or teased into the next corral and the gate closed. As the number of bulls in the main enclosure dwindles the task becomes more diffcult, the animals grow more restless; the last one is always the hardest and sometimes has to be caped through the door. As they move along, gates softly shutting behind them, they find themselves in the last corridor out of which open their individual stalls. All this can be watched in great quiet through openings from above. Everyone who can should enjoy one of these *apartados* as it makes an interesting introduction to the afternoon's spectacle.

Always remembering to save the Alhambra for the ultimate, visit next, as we did, the Generalifé. This was the pleasure palace, the "Garden of Desires," of the Moorish kings. Here, in quiet splendor, they relaxed. On its hilltop overlooking the Alhambra, suspended weightless between land and sky, it rests among its water gardens. I am so ill-informed architecturally that I have to quote my friend Sacherevell Sitwell who compares it to the Villa Lante, my godmother's house in Italy. When I was a child at Lante, like a child I only recalled that Aunt Anita always had candied almonds, but Sitwell with his cunning eye saw it at a later date. To me the Generalifé, though less familiar, is far more romantic. But let me at least quote Sacherevell:

"The sound of waters is as melodious as at Villa Lante. And here are cascades as at Lante or Caprarola, but of Moorish origin, running down the balustrades of a stone stairway (the Moors used these to cool their wrists as they walked up and down the stairs, a charmingly sensuous thought). The loggia—for it would be called that in Italy—has one of the inlaid Moorish ceilings, and there are arabesques upon the walls; but all is simplicity. Its fountains, cy-

presses and arches; for the lovely flower garden is an improvement of our own times. And the view? It is impossible to think of anything more physically beautiful than the view down over Granada and on to the red walls of the Alhambra."

In my experience of the gardens of the Generalifé I can top Sitwell. For once, ten years ago, at the end of those cypress walks with fountains playing from either side into the reflecting pools, lighted by a full moon, Margot Fonteyn danced.

Years later at her house in London I reminisced with her and, though no critic, dared to say it was her loveliest performance. She said, "Jimmy, no one knows oneself what a best performance is, but I promise you no dancer ever danced in surroundings so spectacular, so perhaps you were carried away not by me but by the setting. I only know that I felt I was doing my best." A lovely understatement.

Architecturally the Generalifé is almost nothing, thank God; it is a garden pure and simple, to me the loveliest garden in the world. The Moorish kings were wise. In the Alhambra their artists and their architects were allowed such a free rein that they dazzled you; in the Generalifé they decided to escape into nature. There they could relax from the glut of magnificence; there they could revel in the three things that are the Arabian paradise—greenery, shade and water.

The Arab passion for water, this one element more treasured than jewels by this desert-born race, is so obvious in Granada. Everywhere in Spain you are conscious of their veneration for water, something that in their homeland was so terribly rare. The Arab waterworks all over Andalucía are still in existence. This brings to mind the *"Agua Arabé,"* the Arab water which I use on my farm. I have four wells, all of which I can impound; two feed the garden and the fields, one feeds the house and one the swimming pool, but the Arab water which comes down the great stone ditches, built by them, to my fields I cannot impound. If I can't use it, it flows into the sea. There is a Spanish law, in this most Catholic of countries, which says, "In the eyes of Allah the rich man and the poor man are alike. The rich man can build a cistern and the poor man can not, therefore God's water flows to the rich man and the poor man equally; what can't be used goes to the sea and it is returned to the mountains in clouds for all men's use. No man can trap the gift of Allah."

During our short stay in Granada Greg McIntosh took very few photographs. The subject was too vast, so he intended to come back later and devote days and days to this one inspiring city alone. Naturally he carried a small camera everywhere we went, but it was mostly to take topical shots or pictures as reminders for later work to be done. The whole place, with all its beauties, was well-known to both of us, and we both had a very good preconceived idea of what we wanted. And as I had complete faith in him, there was no point in my interfering in the work of this great artist.

That night we decided to go over and dine in the Parador de San Francisco, which is a must for anyone visiting Granada. This beautiful building, originally a convent, was built by Isabella on the site of a Moorish palace and she used it as her home. I am not sure, but I think she died there. I do know that Ferdinand's and her bodies rested there until the Royal Chapel was completed.

The King outlived the great Queen by so many years, led such a tempestuous, strife-ridden life, both on and off the throne of Spain, regent at times for both his daughter and his grandson, that it is strange to think, as you dine there, of their finally being reunited in this lovely, quiet place.

Exquisitely furnished by the Spanish Government with antiques of the period, it stands in the gardens of the Alhambra and from its terraces gives delightful views of the Albaicín, the Generalifé, the Alhambra itself, and in the background the snowy peaks of the Sierra Nevada, for it faces away from Granada. For fourteen years I have been trying to reserve rooms there without success. It is always full. In fact I have theory that it is occupied year after year by the same groups of visiting old English ladies of great taste. I think I begin to recognize some of the faces.

We dined at eleven, early for Andalucía, and were in bed by one, for at nine o'clock in the morning Pedro Padilla was calling for us to culminate our long voyage. Tomorrow we would visit at last the great monument toward which we had been riding for so many days. Tomorrow the Alhambra!

"To the traveler," wrote Washington Irving, "imbued with a feeling for the historical and poetical, so inseparably intertwined in the annals of romantic Spain, the Alhambra is as much an object of devotion as is the Caaba to all true Moslems. How many legends and traditions, true and fabulous; how many songs, and ballads, Arabian and Spanish, of love and war and chivalry, are associated with this oriental pile! It was the royal abode of the Moorish kings, where, surrounded with splendors and refinements of Asiatic luxury, they held dominion over what they vaunted as a terrestrial paradise, and made their last stand for empire in Spain. The royal palace forms but a part of a fortress, the walls of which, studded with towers, stretch irregularly round the whole crest of a hill, a spur of the Sierra Navada or Snowy Mountains, and overlook the city; externally it is a rude congregation of towers and battlements, with no regularity of plan nor grace of architecture, and giving little promise of the grace and beauty which prevail within."

I disagree somewhat with the great writer when he speaks of lack of plan and architecture, for to me one of the beauties of the Alhambra is that the enormous walls follow the entire contour of the hill on which it stands. It is not set on its hill; it grows out of it, a great work of Man embellishing a great monument of

Nature. Those red walls seem endless, soaring majestically above the forest through which they are approached.

When you come to the entrance of this huge place you are immediately made conscious of its original purpose, for you are faced by no impressive portal, no magnificent *entrada;* this approach was not intended to welcome but repel. You walk in, now as then, through a narrow barbican, the only way to the hilltop, which twists and turns, defensible by a few men against hundreds. This narrow passageway opens after about a hundred yards into the vast forecourt of the fort. This is called the Plaza de los Algibes or cisterns, for underfoot, cut in the living rock, is the immense water supply, fed by conduits from the mountains, which were sufficient to supply a garrison of twenty thousand men over a siege of weeks. Around three sides stand buildings which were barracks and storehouses, stables and armories. On your right is the palace proper entered by a great portal, an immense Arab arch of horseshoe form which springs to half the height of the tower. This is the Gate of Justice, so called from the law that used to be dispensed there; this typical Moslem custom of dispensing judgement from the gates, which still prevails across the Mediterranean, is alluded to in the sacred Scriptures, "Judges and officers shalt thou make thee in all thy gates and they shall judge the people." Within the vestibule is sculptured a gigantic hand, and further in an equally large key. The hand is the emblem of doctrine; the five fingers signify the five commandments of Islam—fasting, pilgrimage, charity, ablution, and war against the infidels, the key is the emblem of fate, the key of Daoud or King David, transmitted to the Prophet Mohammed. "And the key of the House of David will I lay upon his shoulder; so he shall open and none shall shut, and he shall shut and none shall open" (Isaiah XXII), for the prophets of the Old Testament are also the prophets of Islam.

The courtyard and the vestibule are now cluttered with gypsies selling castanets, and there is one rather good gift shop run by a member of the Linares' family who also own the best antique shops in Madrid, Granada, and Sevilla. Linares prices are high everywhere, but they are utterly to be trusted, their word is their bond.

At this point I want to diverge a moment on the subject of guides. There are always licensed guides at the Alhambra, as there are everywhere in Spain. Their prices are regulated and they are all absolutely capable on their particular subject. I have found, however, that one can be much more pleasantly informed by arranging for a guide through the hotel concierge. Many of their guides are young gentlemen working their way through college, serious students of history, of architecture, of the antique, and rather than mumbling by rote a given set of speeches they take a vivid interest in their subjects. Instead of an automatic tour you find yourself accompanied by an intellectual friend who can make your visit infinitely more enjoyable.

I don't know where I got the idea that Washington Irving on his arrival at Granada found the Alhambra in a ruined state and occupied by gypsies and smugglers; I do know that it is a rather commonly held piece of misinformation and I want to take this opportunity to correct it. After the kingdom had passed into the hands of the Christians, the Alhambra continued to be a royal demesne and was occasionally occupied by Spanish kings on their visits to the south. In fact the Emperor Charles V tore down the old winter palace of the Moorish kings and commenced to build a sumptuous Renaissance palace of white stone in its place. It has a very beautiful circular court by Pedro Machuca; the lower storey is Doric, the upper Ionic. Charles intended the courtyard to be the scene of tournaments and the mounted bullfights that were popular in his day; repeated earthquakes, however, discouraged the Emperor and his architect so that they were afraid to carry the building any higher than the second floor, and there it stands, a Renaissance monument of great purity smack in the middle of all the Moorish splendor. It may sound like an anachronism, but Sitwell finds it an interesting contrast. "There comes a time when sooner than stand again in the Hall of the Abencerrages or the Hall of the Two Sisters, we find ourselves admiring the unfinished Palace of Charles V nearby. It is now used as the handsome setting for concerts in the summertime."

However, the last royal visitors were Philip V and his queen, Elizabeth of Parma, very early in the eighteenth century. At that time both the palace and the gardens were completely restored, mostly by architects and gardeners that the Queen brought over from Italy; it may have been these men who gave the Generalifé its *Italianate* quality. The royal visit, however, was brief and the place once more became neglected. The Military Governor of Granada and his garrison moved in; it reverted to a barracks. Its beautiful halls became desolate, the gardens were destroyed, the fountains ceased to play. It was at this time that a populace of beggars, gypsies, *contrabandistas,* all the riff-raff of Granada, moved into the ruins.

This sad state of affairs persisted until the French occupation when Granada, through the fortunes of war, fell into the hands of the invader. This was a very terrible time for the inhabitants of Spain but, as it turned out, a very fortunate thing for the magnificent ruins. The French garrisoned the Alhambra to secure themselves from the bitter populace; the French commandant, evidently a man of taste, took up his quarters in the palace. I quote from Irving again:

"With that enlightened taste that has ever distinguished the French Nation in their conquests, this monument of Moorish elegance and grandeur was rescued from the absolute ruin and desolation that was overwhelming it. The roofs were repaired, the saloons and galleries protected from the weather, the gardens cultivated, the watercourses restored, the fountains once more made to throw up their sparkling showers; and Spain may thank her invaders for having preserved for her the most beautiful and interesting of her historical monuments."

Irving continues: "I cannot conclude this brief notice of the state of the fortress without bearing testimony to the honorable exertions of its present commander, Don Francisco de Serna, who is tasking all the limited sources at his command to keep the palace in a state of repair, and by his judicious precautions has for some time arrested its too certain decay."

So you see Washington Irving must have found it in pretty good condition.

I have mentioned the two halls of the Abencerrages and the Two Sisters. I find them most typical examples of the Alhambra architecture in that all the decoration of importance is in the ceilings. These consist of stalactite pendentives completely covered with the interlocking honeycomb cells so typical of the building; the ceilings seem to drip down from the roof. The contrast in the Alhambra between the simplicity of its columns, which carry your eye up to these impalpable ceilings, is impossible to describe; they seem not to support these ornate superstructures but to hang from them.

You enter the palace proper through a great courtyard centered by a reflecting pool a hundred and twenty-four feet long and twenty-seven wide. Passing from this, through a Moorish archway, you come directly into the famous Court of the Lions, probably the most famous patio in the world. Round its sides are light Moorish colonnades of open filigree work supported by slender pillars of white marble. These were originally gold-plated. The whole effect is light and elegant; the fragile fretwork, combined with the airy honeycombed ceilings, makes it one of the most suave settings for a fountain imaginable. The Moors always preferred elegance to grandeur, and this is certainly the most elegant courtyard in the world. The twelve famous lions that support the alabaster fountain in the center disappointed Washington Irving. They are very crude and primitive and he thought "unworthy of their fame, being of miserable sculpture, the work probably of some Christian captive." Actually their source is unknown. You see the same type in some parts of Italy. They may be Norman, the spoils of some earlier war. My untutored guess is that they are early Saracenic. At any rate, with impeccable taste, the builders of this patio chose these crude figures to contrast and enhance the delicacy of their surroundings.

I beg you here to indulge me in a long quotation from Washington Irving which expresses not only my feelings but those of many people familiar with the early history of Spain. It was here in this very courtyard that he was led to philosophize:

"As I sat watching the effect of the declining daylight . . . I was led into a consideration of the light, elegant, and voluptuous character, prevalent throughout its internal architecture; and to contrast it with the grand but gloomy solemnity of the Gothic edifices reared by the Spanish conquerors. The very architecture thus bespeaks the opposite and irreconcilable natures of the two warlike people who so long battled here for the mastery of the peninsula. By degrees I fell into a course of musing upon the singular fortunes of the Arabian or Morisco-Spaniards, whose whole existence is as a tale that is told, and certainly forms one of the most anomalous yet splendid episodes in history. Potent and durable as was their dominion, we scarcely know how to call them. They were a nation without a legitimate country or name. A remote wave of the great Arabian inundation, cast upon the shores of Europe, they seemed to have all the impetus of the first rush of the torrent. Their career of conquest, from the Rock of Gibraltar to the cliffs of the Pyrenees, was as rapid and brilliant as the Moslem victories of Syria and Egypt. Nay, had they not been checked on the plains of Tours, all France, all Europe, might have been overrun with the same facility as the empires of the East, and the Crescent at this day have glittered on the fanes of Paris and London.

"Repelled within the limits of the Pyrenees, the mixed hordes of Asia and Africa, that formed this great eruption, gave up the Moslem principle of conquest, and sought to establish in Spain a peaceful and permanent dominion. As conquerors, their heroism was only equalled by their moderation; and in both, for a time, they excelled the nations with whom they contended. Severed from their native homes, they loved the land given them as they supposed by Allah, and strove to embellish it with everything that could administer to the happiness of man. Laying the foundations of their power in a system of wise and equitable laws, diligently cultivating the arts and sciences, and promoting agriculture, manufactures, and commerce, they gradually formed an empire unrivalled for its prosperity by any of the empires of Christendom; and diligently drawing round them the graces and refinements which marked the Arabian empire in the East at the time of its greatest civilization, they diffused the light of oriental knowledge through the western regions of benighted Europe.

"The cities of Arabian Spain became the resort of Christian artisans, to instruct themselves in the useful arts. The universities of Toledo, Córdoba, Seville, and Granada were sought by the pale student from other lands to acquaint himself with the sciences of the Arabs, and the treasured lore of antiquity; the lovers of the gay science resorted to Córdoba and Granada, to imbibe the poetry and music of the East; and the steel-clad warriors of the North hastened thither to accomplish themselves in the graceful exercises and courteous usages of chivalry.

"And now a few broken monuments are all that remain to bear witness to eight hundred years of power and dominion, as solitary rocks, left far in the interior, bear testimony to the extent of some vast inundation. Such is the Alhambra. A Moslem pile in the midst of a Christian land; an oriental palace amidst the Gothic edifices of the West; an elegant memento of a brave, intelligent, and graceful people, who conquered, ruled, flourished and passed away."

Reading this, I can only reflect that the Goths from whom we are descended worshiped the North Wind and the Naked Sword. Of course they later dropped the North Wind for the Cross, but they never gave up their worship of the Sword; but the Arabs only reverenced Allah and intellect. You all know who won.

From the Hall of the Ambassadors, which is pierced on three sides by windows, one gets the finest views from the Alhambra overlooking Granada, the Albaicín and, on the other side, a magnificent vista to the Sierra Nevada. This majestically proportioned room held the throne of the king. Here all business was transacted, emissaries received; from here he ruled his empire.

It is a perfect square set in the exact center of the castle, occupying the whole interior of the Tower of Comáres; fifty feet from wall to wall, it is sixty-five feet high, culminating in a superb domed ceiling of cedar wood with a pattern of hundreds of polygons and intersecting lines. Although the ceiling is almost lost in the obscurity of its great height, one can still see remnants of the rich gilding and the brilliant reds and blues with which it was once picked out. Opposite the entrance is a large alcove in which, up a few steps, stood the royal throne. The back of this alcove is covered with arabesques describing the history of Yusef I who completed this great palace. They say that the Emperor Charles V, on his first sight of this grand chamber, walked silently around, looking out of the windows at the glorious prospects, finally turning to his courtiers and saying, "Unhappy the man who lost all this."

If you step through the windows onto the balcony facing the mountains you can see the hill called La Cuesta de las Lagrimas, the Hill of Tears, the route by which Boabdil the last King of Granada, fled with the remnants of his court. Beyond it rises another eminence where he paused and turned to take a last view of the paradise from which he had been expelled. This spot is called El Ultimo Suspiro del Moro, the Last Sigh of the Moor. His mother, the Princess Ayxa, seeing him weeping, said scornfully, "You do well to weep as a woman over what you could not defend as a man!" Not very consoling.

The afternoon light was beginning to slant enough to give Greg shadows that he wanted for his photography, so I left him there and went back to the hotel. There were a few things left to do in wrapping up the loose ends of the trip.

Arranging for the trucking of the horses and men back to Jerez and telephoning to Marbella to send a car to fetch us home took quite a little time. By the time these chores were taken care of my photographer turned up. It seemed that, incurably romantic, Greg had tried to get permission to spend the night in Washington Irving's bed. Of course he was refused but consoled himself with the remark that it seemed damned small and far less comfortable than the Alhambra Palace Hotel, to say nothing of the total lack of plumbing.

While on the subject of Granada I want to mention a wonderful restaurant that I do not think is in most of the tourist guides. The Capilla Réal, containing the tombs of Ferdinand and Isabella, opens onto a most beautiful Gothic square. The Chapel, the Cathedral and the Palace of the Archbishop form three sides of this magnificent plaza. At night soft illumination lights their intricate façades. On the fourth side stands a wonderful little café oddly named the Bar Sevilla. Weather permitting, its tables spill out into this magic plaza, and there Greg and I dined royally on the specialties of the house, omelet Sacro Monte and chicken grilled with whisky and garlic. The omelet, a concoction of calves brains, is a gypsy dish and named after the hill in Granada where their caves are located. This little gem of a restaurant is very popular with Granadeños, very small, always crowded, and a table must be reserved. *"Buen provecho!"* Good appetite.

At certain seasons of the year the Alhambra is now illuminated with great taste, imagination and restraint. A year ago Pedro Padilla had taken me and my wife up to a little square in the Moorish town across the valley from the Alhambra. You walk to a balustrade at the edge of a cliff and across the valley you see, gently lighted, those great rose-colored walls which seem to stretch out of sight on either side. Here and there the forests that lead up to it are lighted, and suddenly you look down at your feet and there, brightly illuminated but the size of a postage stamp, is one of the principal squares of Granada. You look from that back up at those soaring battlements and you get a sense of their proportion; you realize, as in no other way, the immensity and majesty with which the Moors built. They were here for over seven hundred years; they left their influence indelibly all over Spain. This was their final signature.

# FATE

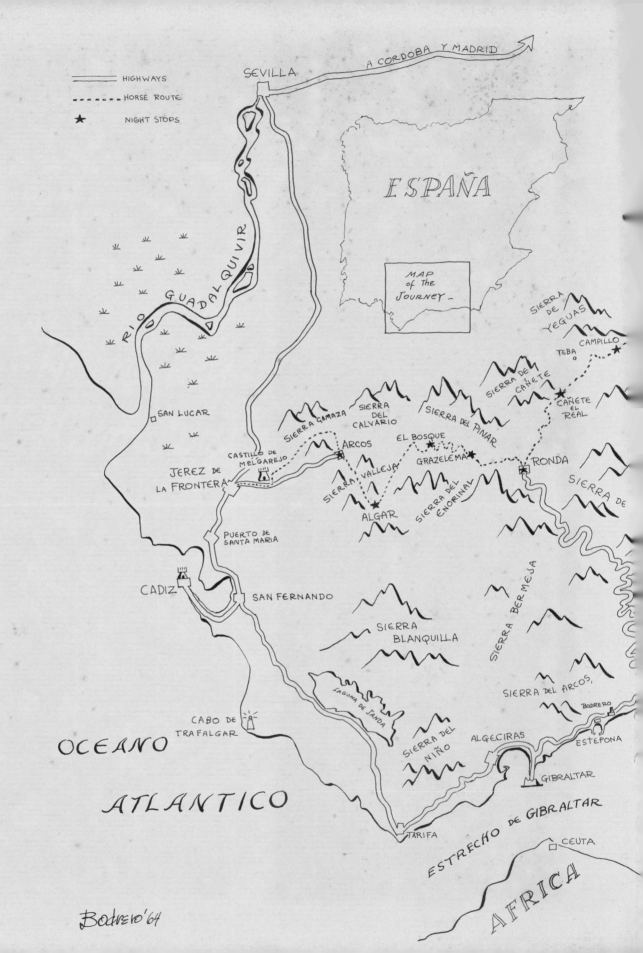